At *Ladies' Home Journal*, we chronicled the story of Diana for the past sixteen years. Many of us remember waking up at four-thirty in the morning to watch her, a shy and rosy bride, exchange vows with her Prince.

She grew up before our eyes, evolving from the sweet young Princess trying to learn the ways of the royals to a mother whose love for her sons was so apparent and so intense, it reminded us all of our passion for our own children.

And then suddenly, the story changed; the fairy tale was not what it seemed. We used the name of *Ladies' Home Journal*'s most popular column as the headline for a report on Diana and Charles: "Can This Marriage Be Saved?" For this mismatched couple, it just couldn't.

Still, Diana went on, sometimes painfully

but with increasing strength, to create a life for herself, focusing on what was most important to her: guiding her sons to maturity and helping those in need.

The last piece the *Journal* published about Diana reported on her commitment to abolishing land mines and aiding land-mine victims. In it, we described her as elegant, witty and newly self-confident.

And then came the tragic news of Diana's death. Once again we awoke in the early morning hours—this time to watch the funeral of a woman who seemed like a friend who had died much too young. It was a very painful and personal loss.

In this special *Journal* tribute, we celebrate the life of Diana and the legacy of love she left behind.

A portion of the proceeds from the sale of this publication will go to The Diana, Princess of Wales Memorial Fund.

Mummy

"I do so love my boys"

"I want to be
a policeman
so I can look
after you,
Mummy."

—Prince William

CLOCKWISE FROM LEFT: P. LEDRU/SYGMA; TIM GRAHAM/SYGMA; GAMMA LIAISON; TIM GRAHAM/SYGMA

15

"I want to bring them up with security. I hug my children to death..."

"I will fight for my children on any level in order for them to be happy and have peace of mind and carry out their duties."

"If you see her with her two beautiful, charming children, you can see that she's happy."

— Earl Spencer,
Diana's father

"The rest of us have lost a superstar and a very important ambassador. But the children have lost

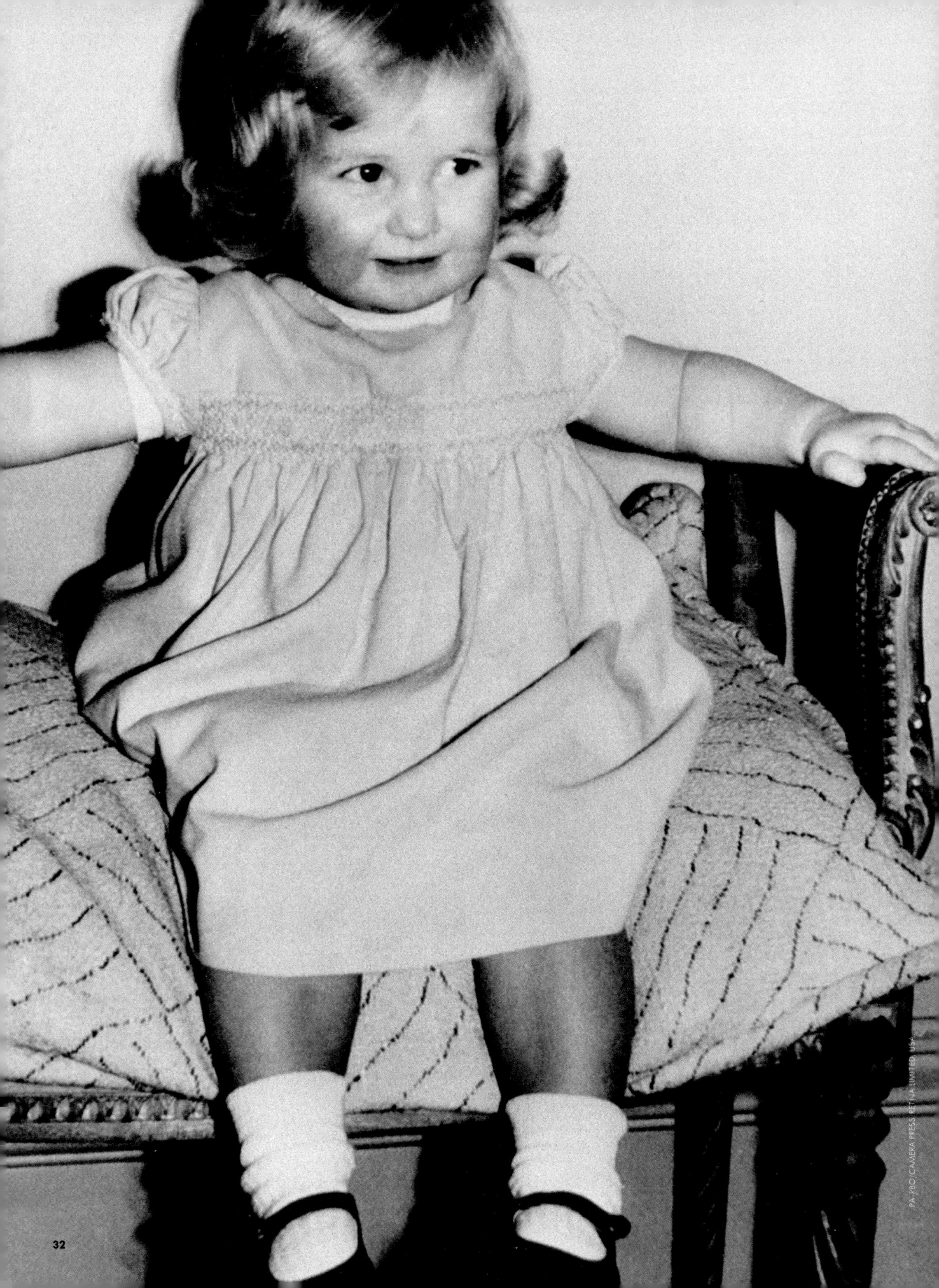

A
Very
British
Girl

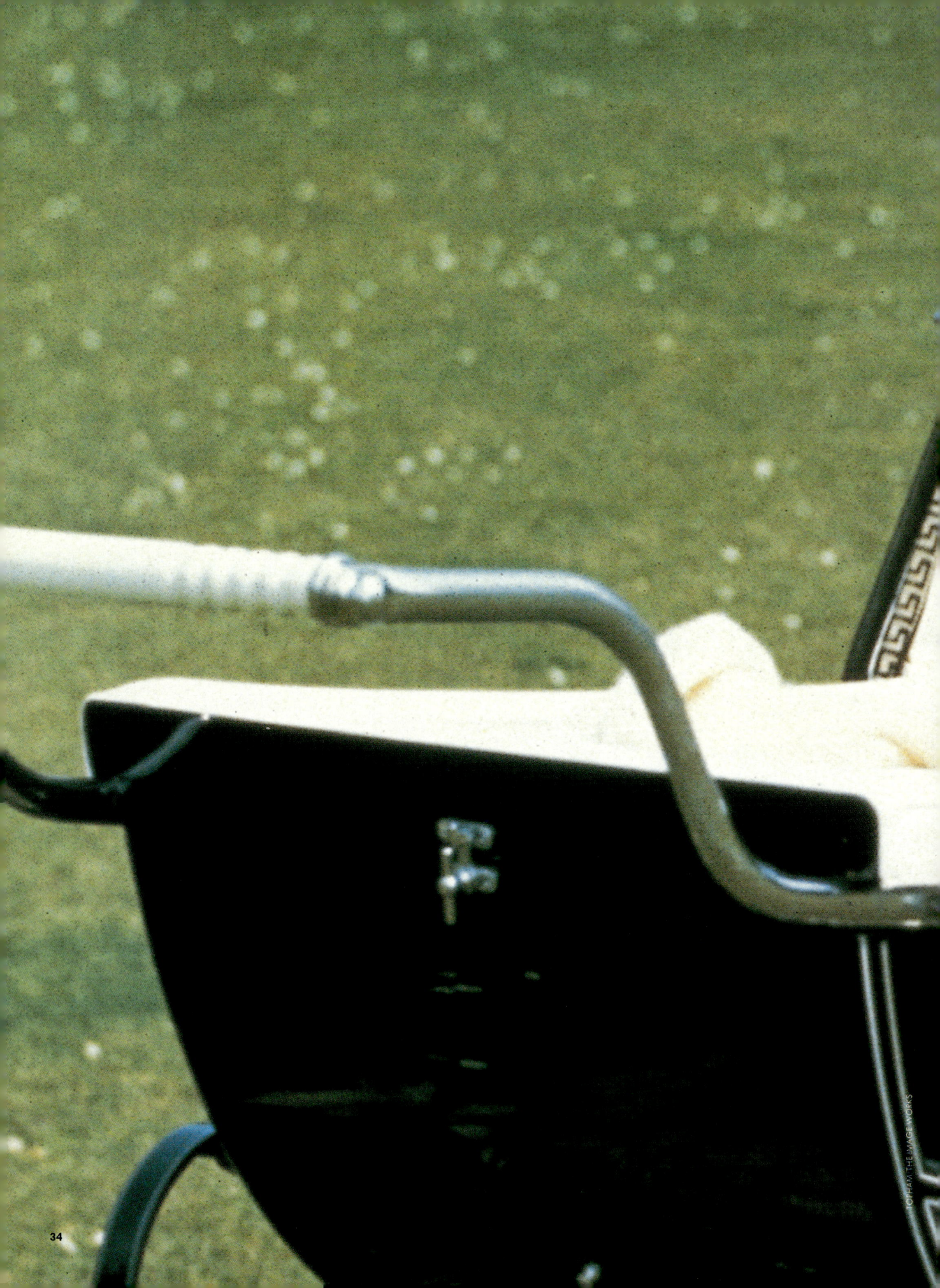

"She hadn't changed from the big sister who mothered me as a baby…"

—Earl Spencer, Diana's brother

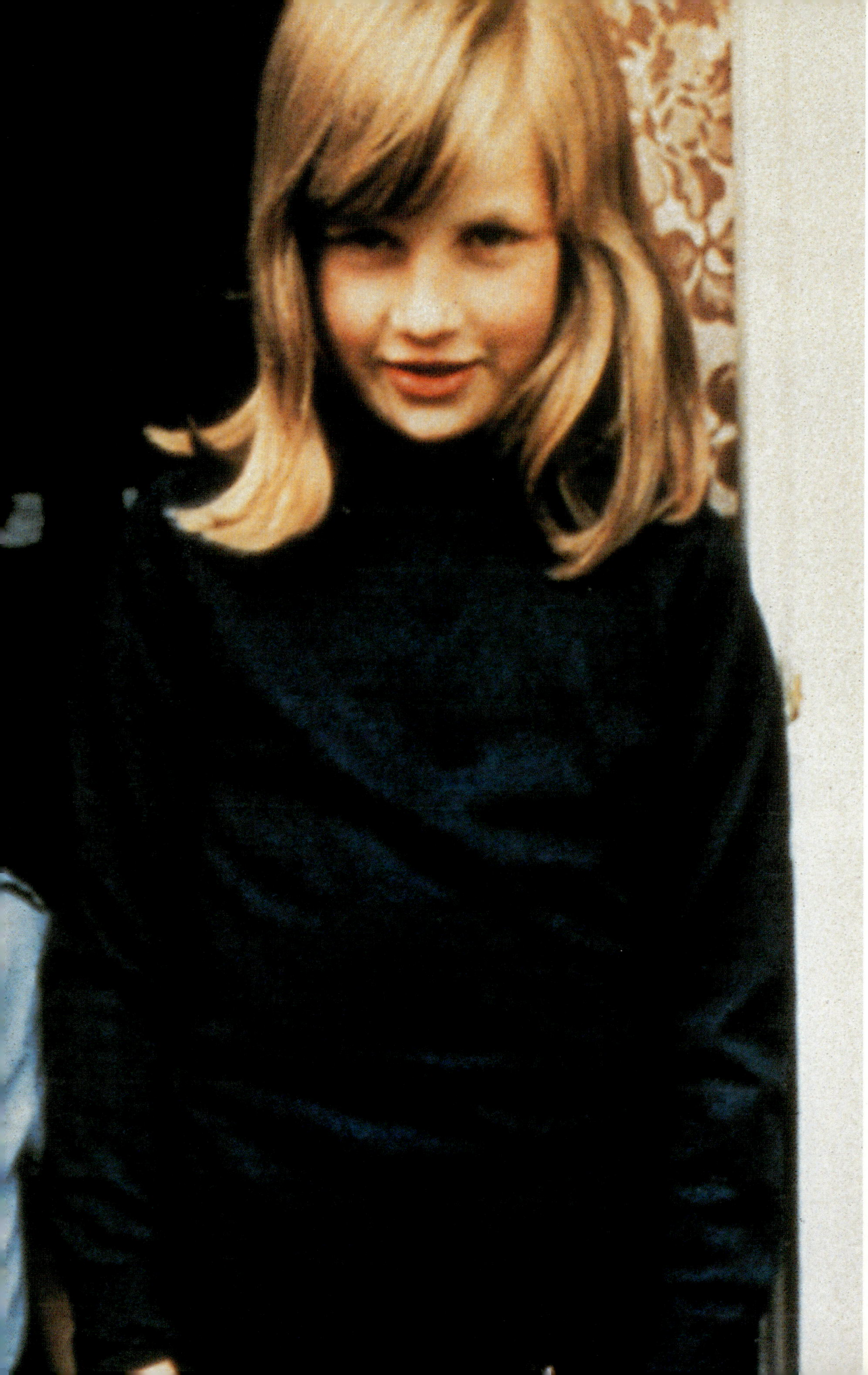

*"I thank God
for the gift
of Diana..."*

—Frances Shand Kydd,
Diana's mother

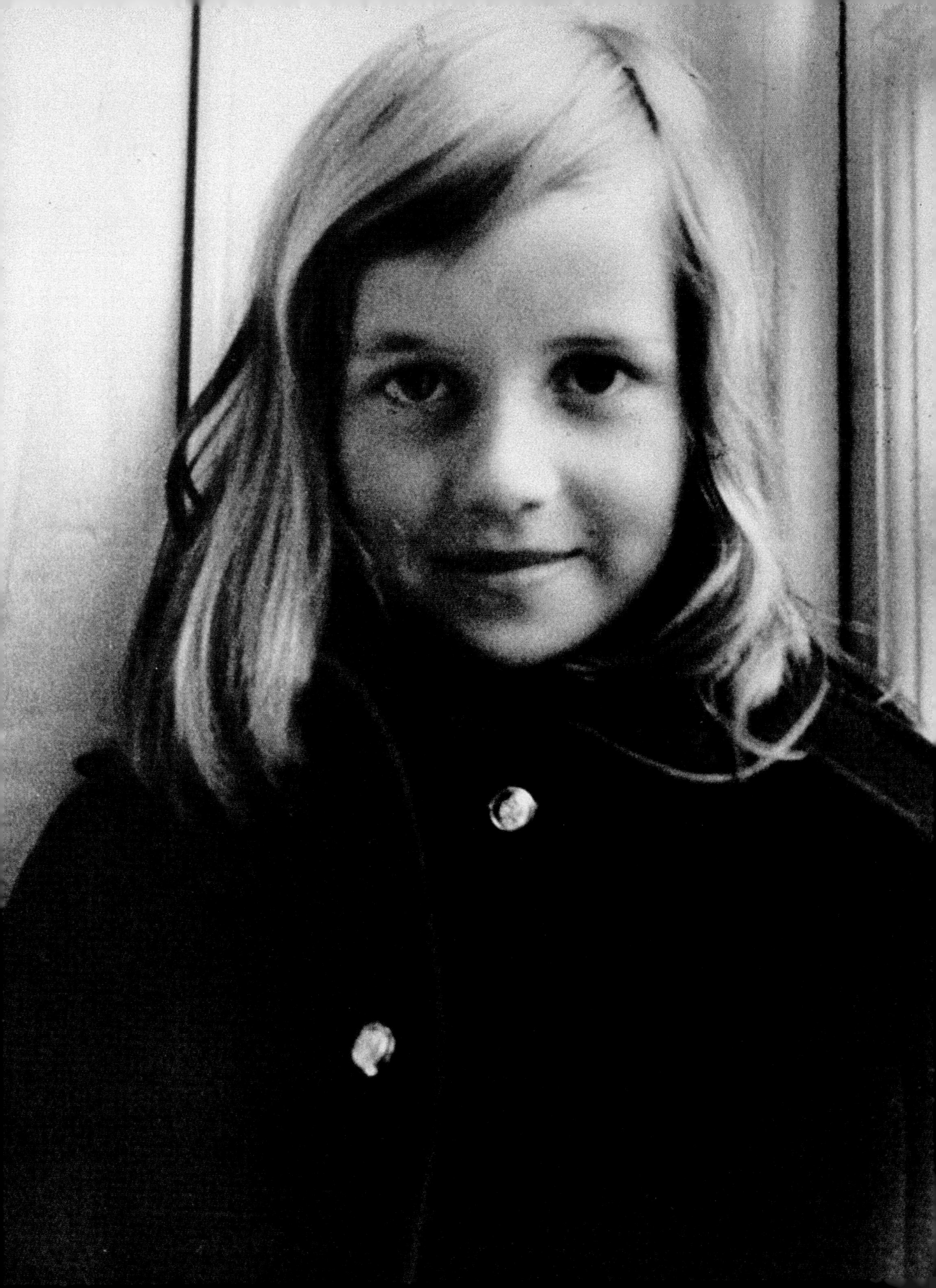

"I want to be

or the Princ

a dancer—

ess of Wales."

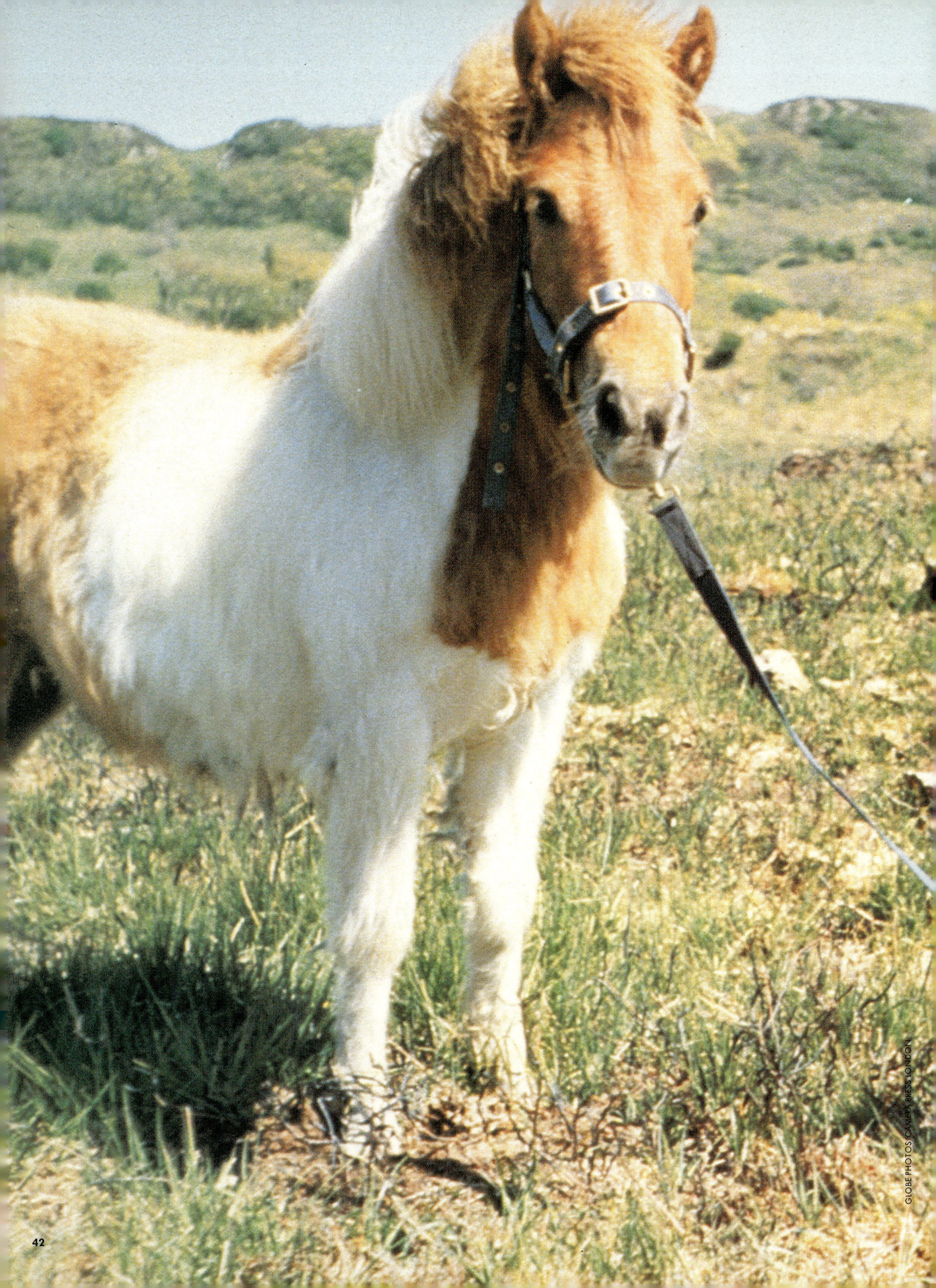

GLOBE PHOTOS/CAMERA PRESS LONDON

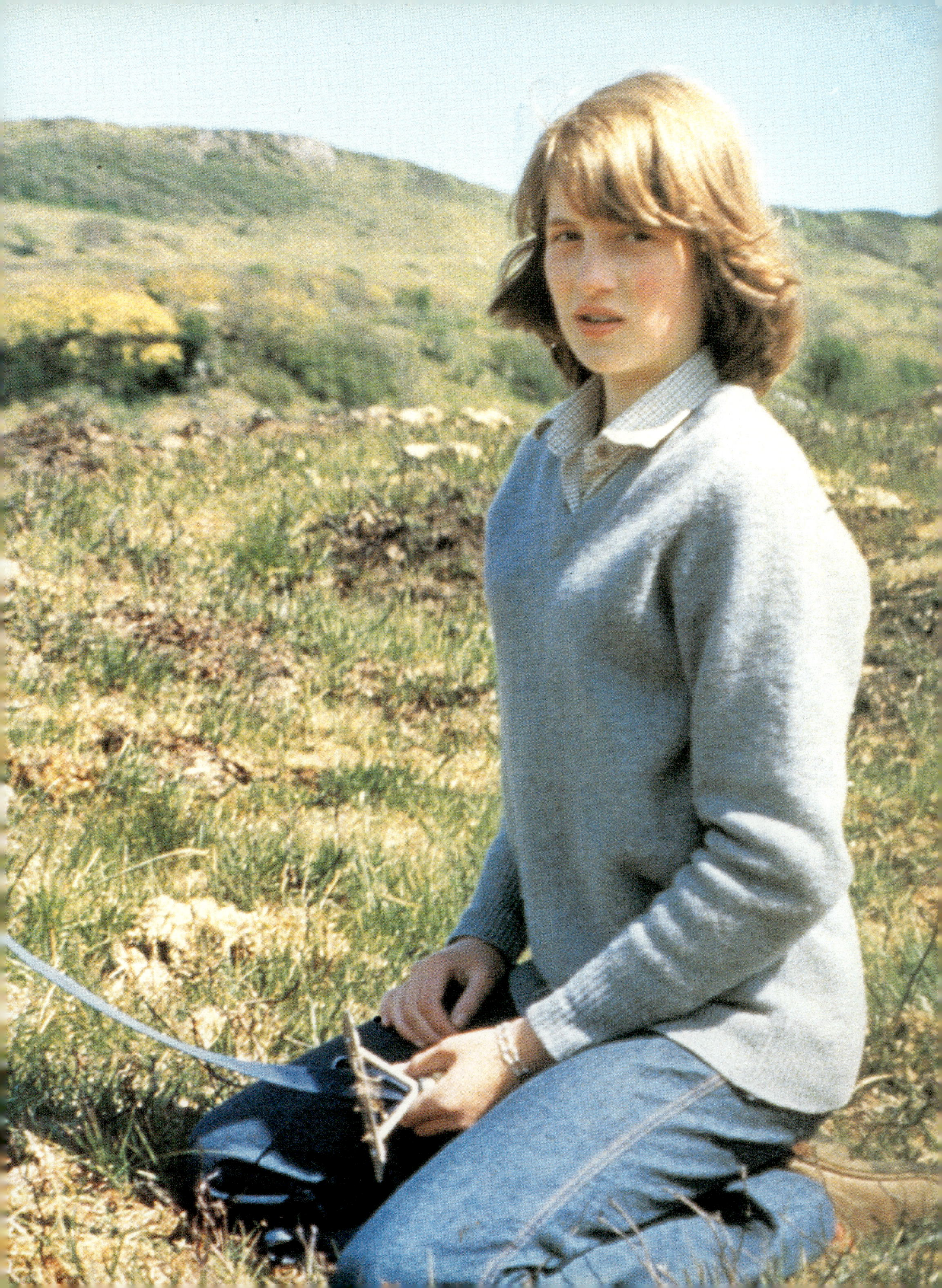

"At the age of nineteen, you always think you're prepared for everything, and you think you have the knowledge of what's coming ahead."

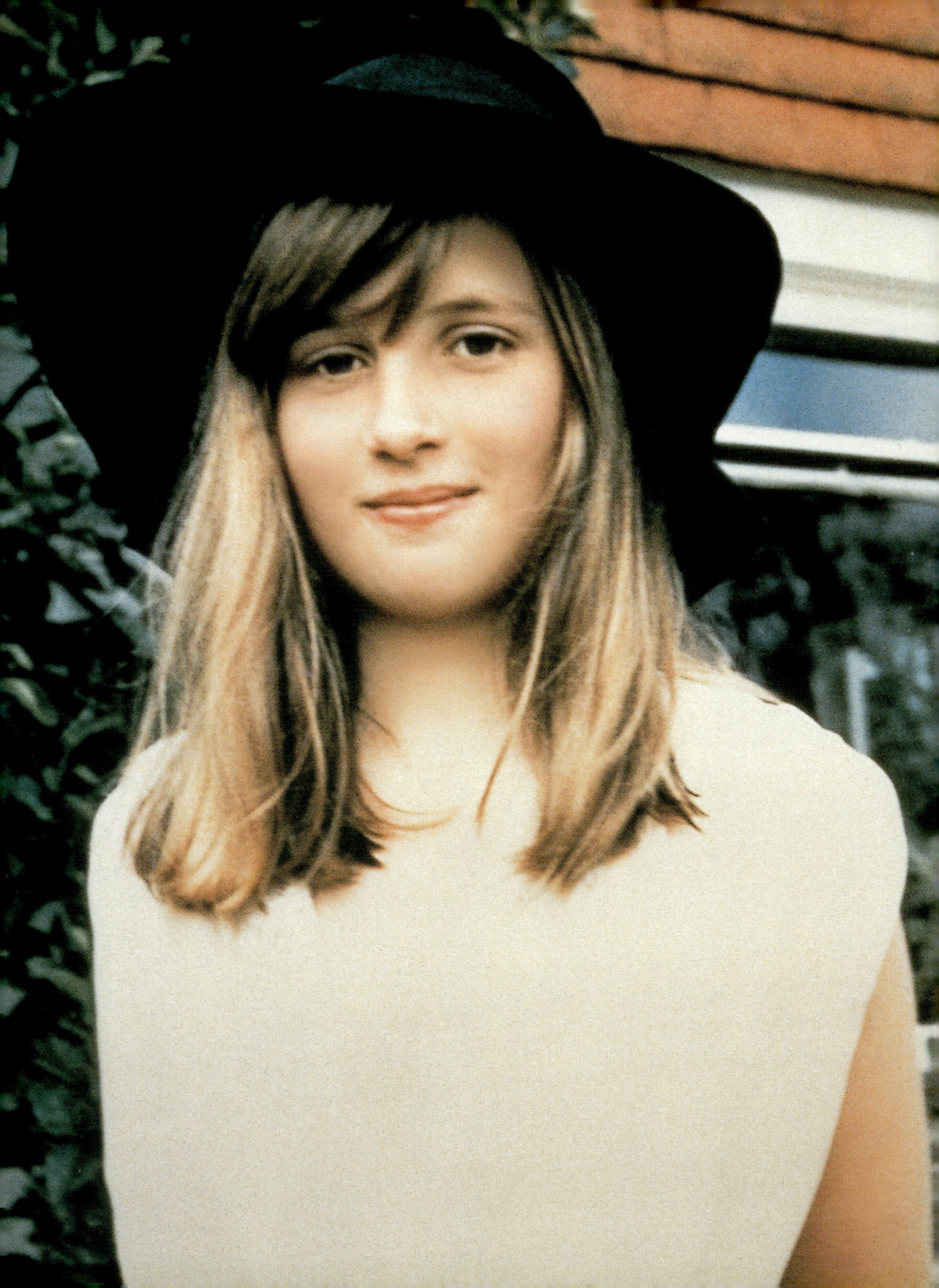

"One minute I was a nobody, the next minute I was the Princess of Wales…"

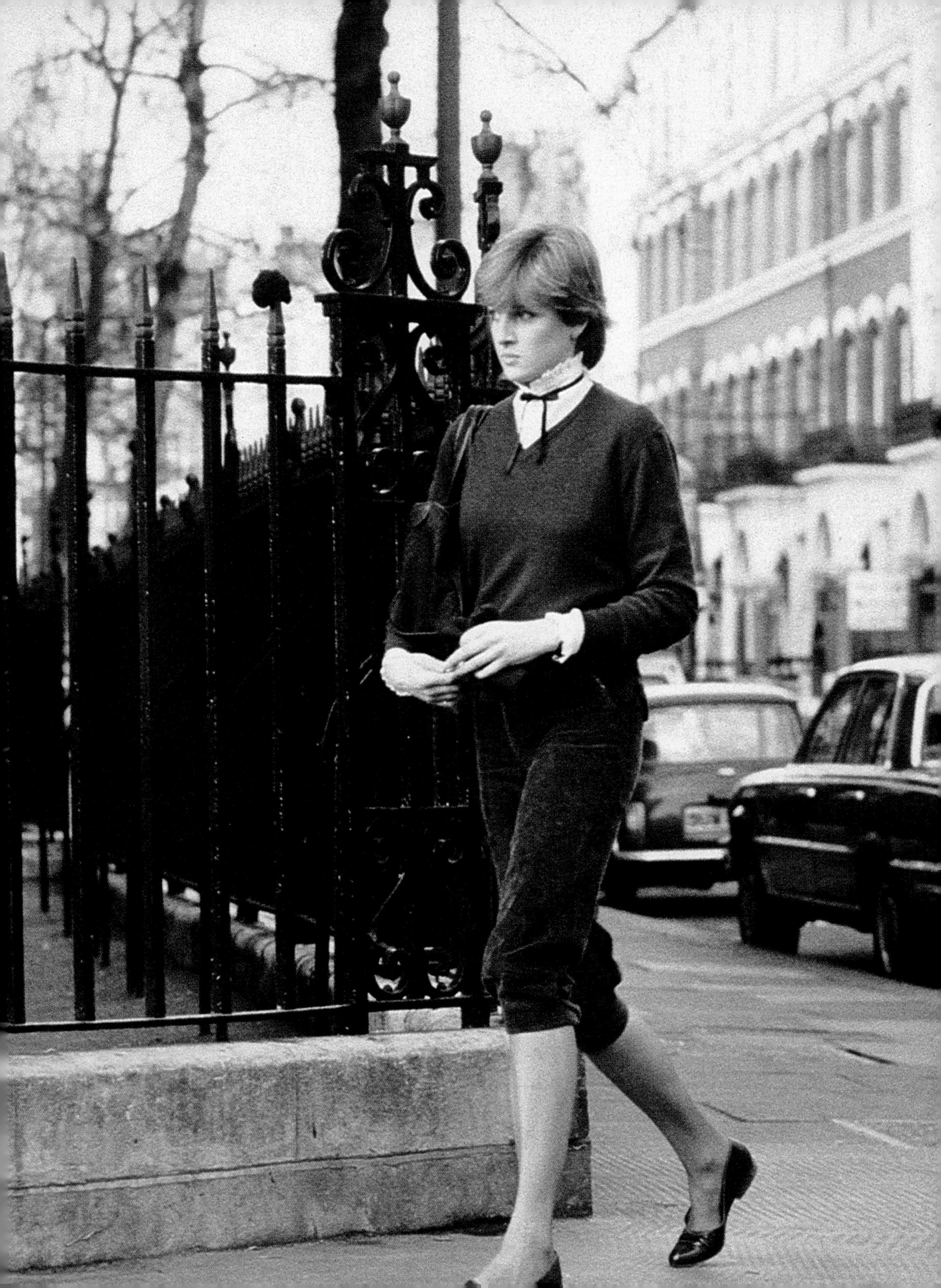

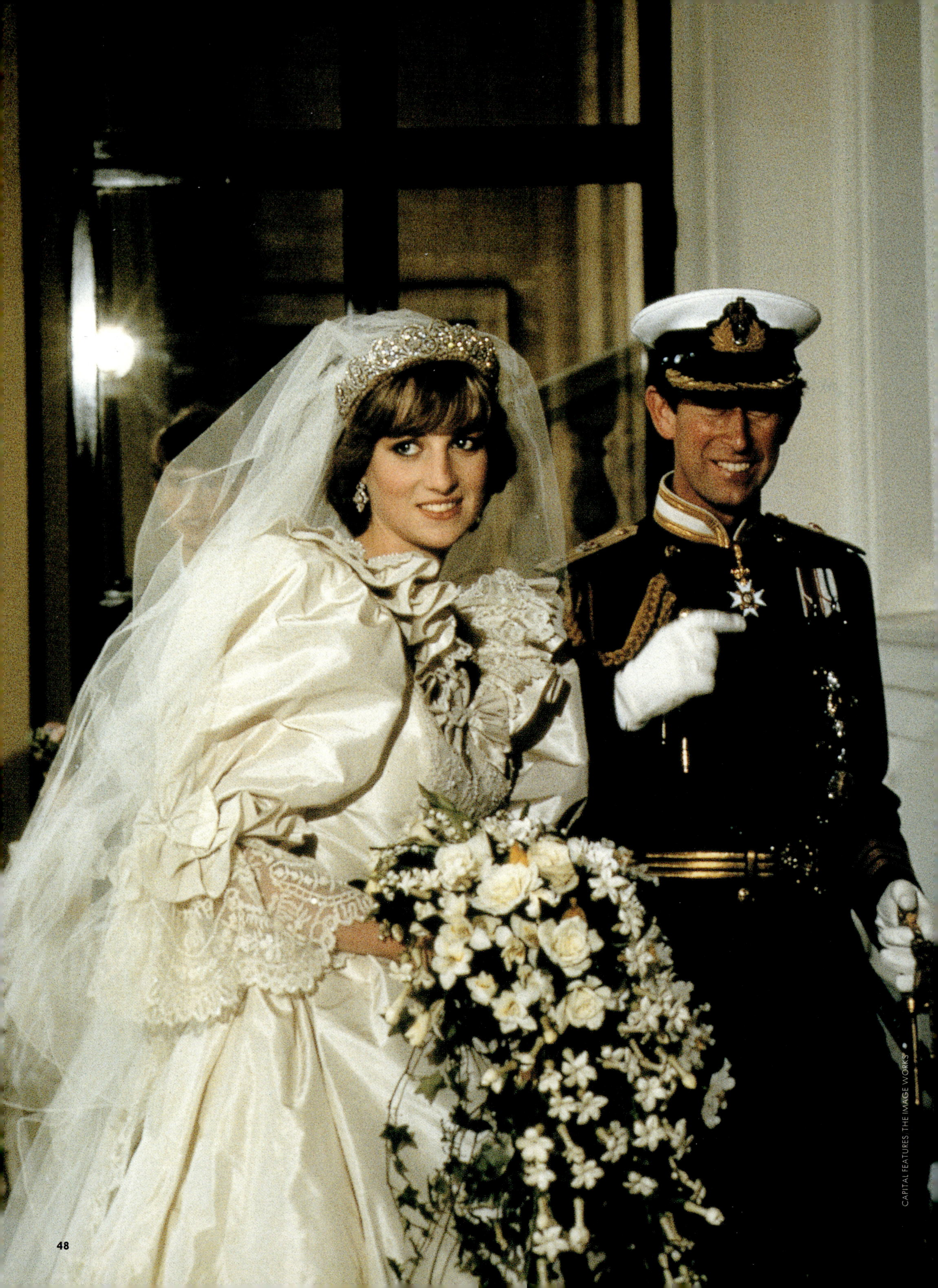

CAPITAL FEATURES THE IMAGE WORKS

Princess of Wales

"With Charles beside me, I cannot go wrong."

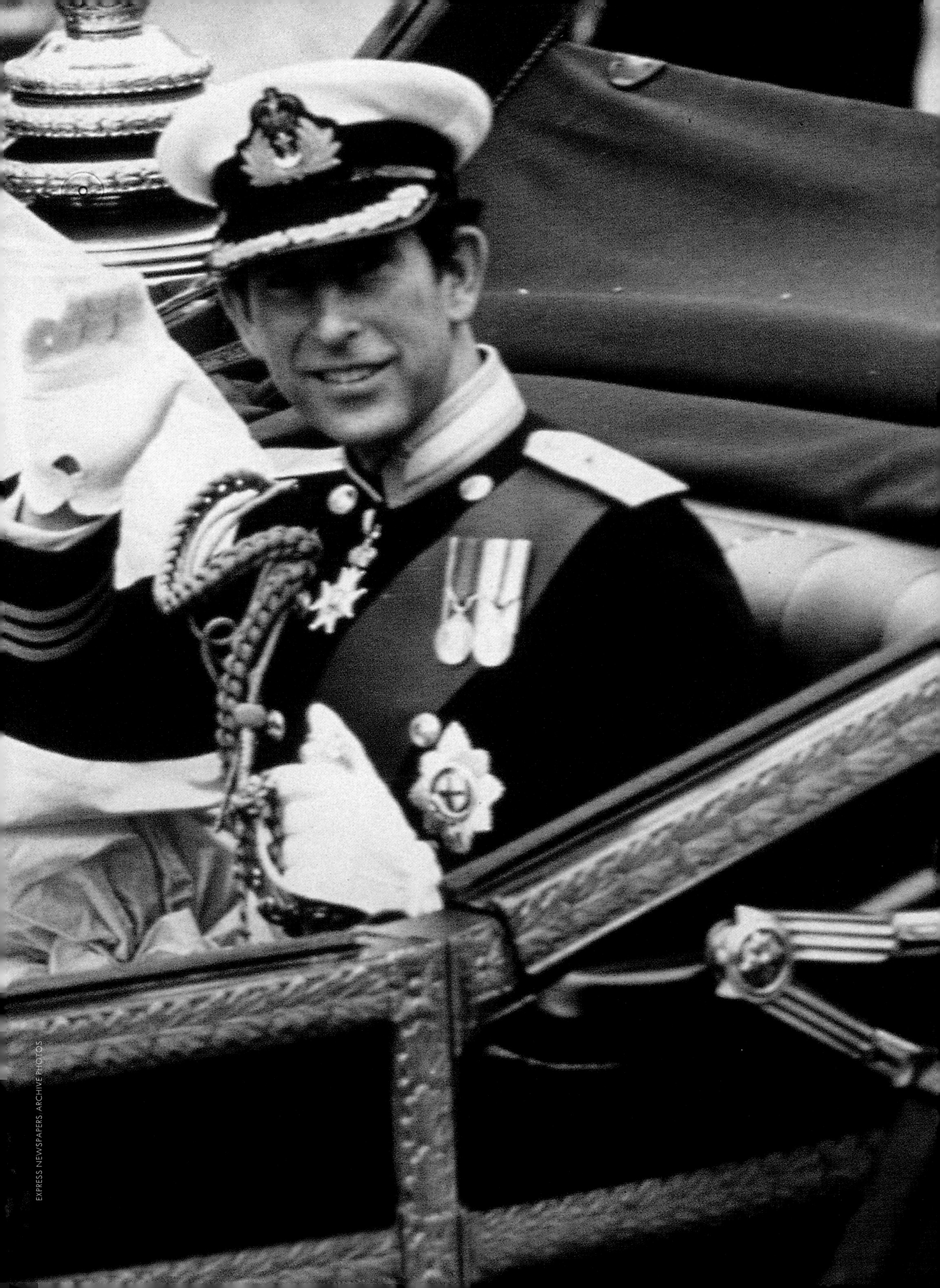

EXPRESS NEWSPAPERS ARCHIVE PHOTOS

52

CLOCKWISE FROM LEFT: PATRICK LICHFIELD/GLOBE PHOTOS; GLOBE PHOTOS; SYGMA

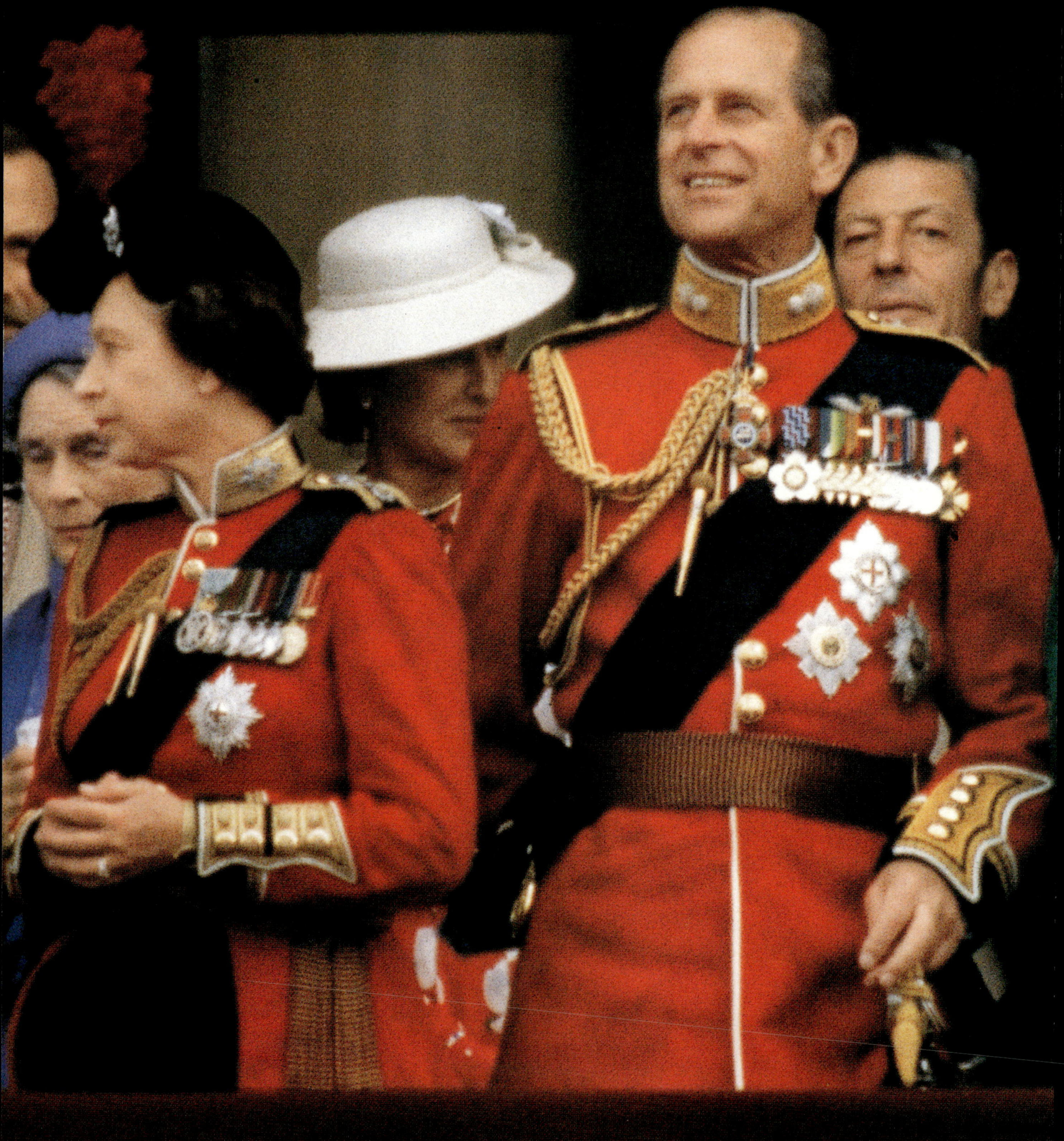

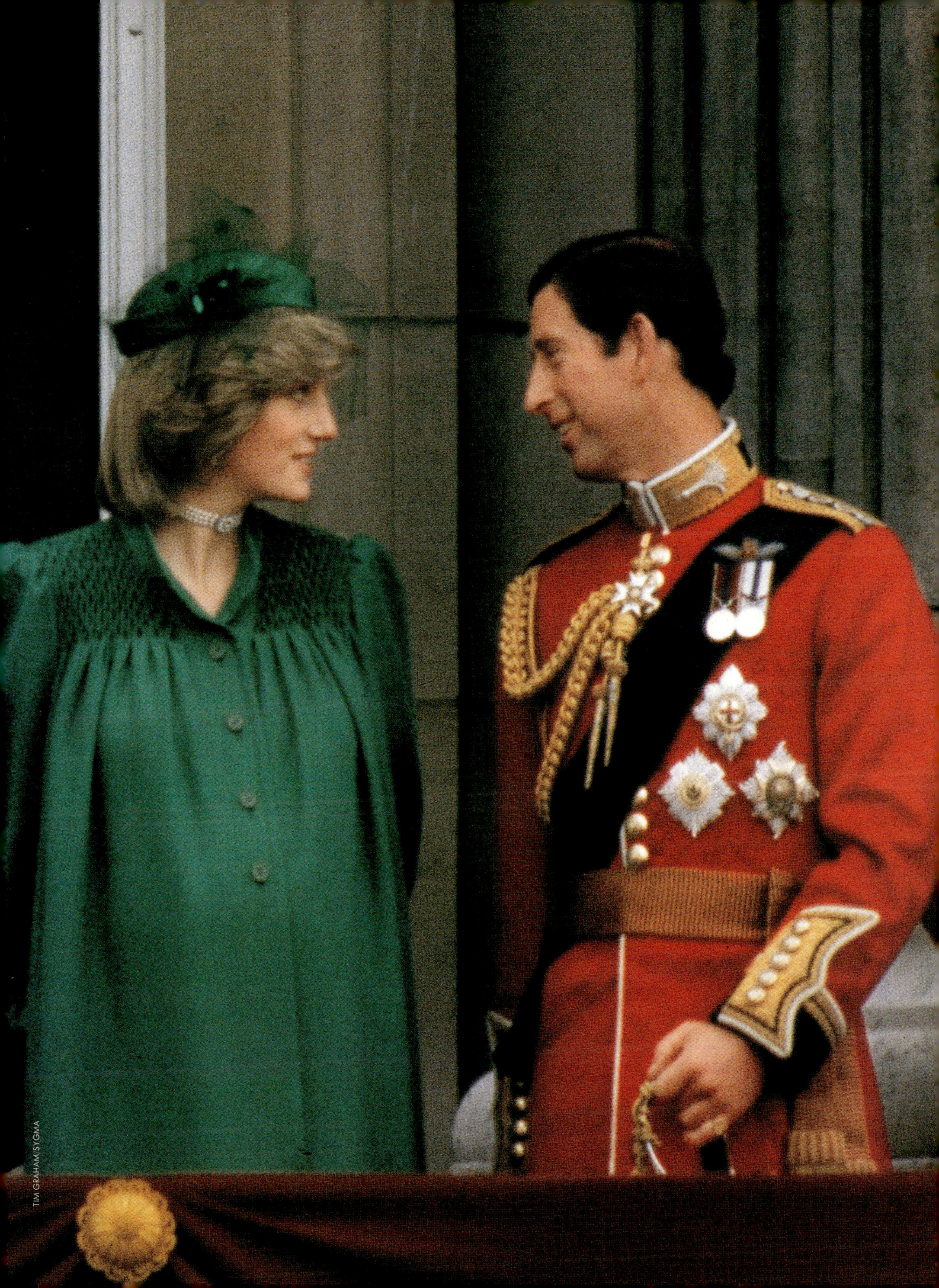

TIM GRAHAM/SYGMA

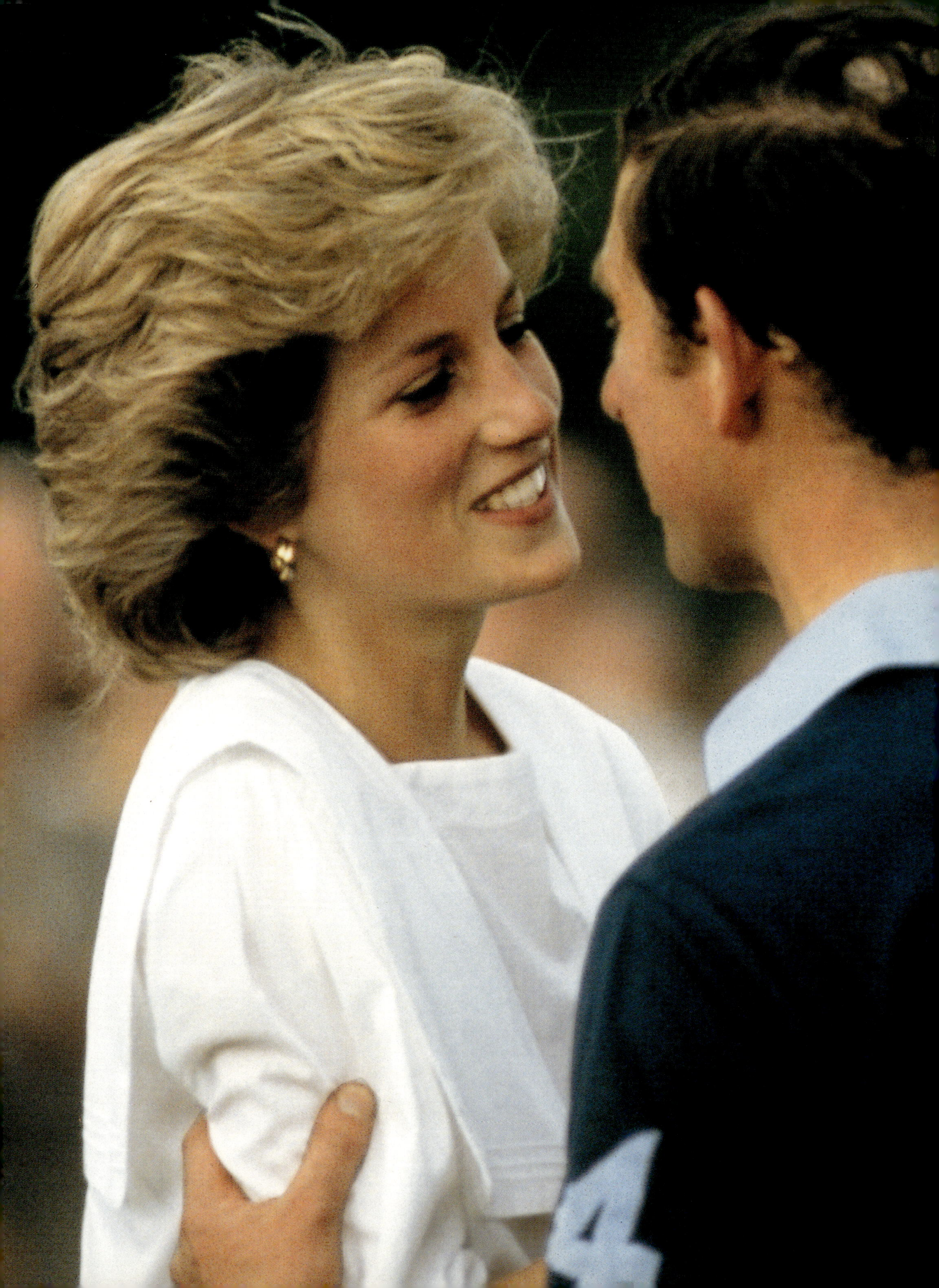

"I remember thinking... great fun and bouncy and full of life."

—*Prince Charles*

CLOCKWISE FROM LEFT: TIM GRAHAM/SYGMA, LONDON FEATURES.

"I desperately loved my husband, and I wanted to share everything together. I thought that we were a very good team."

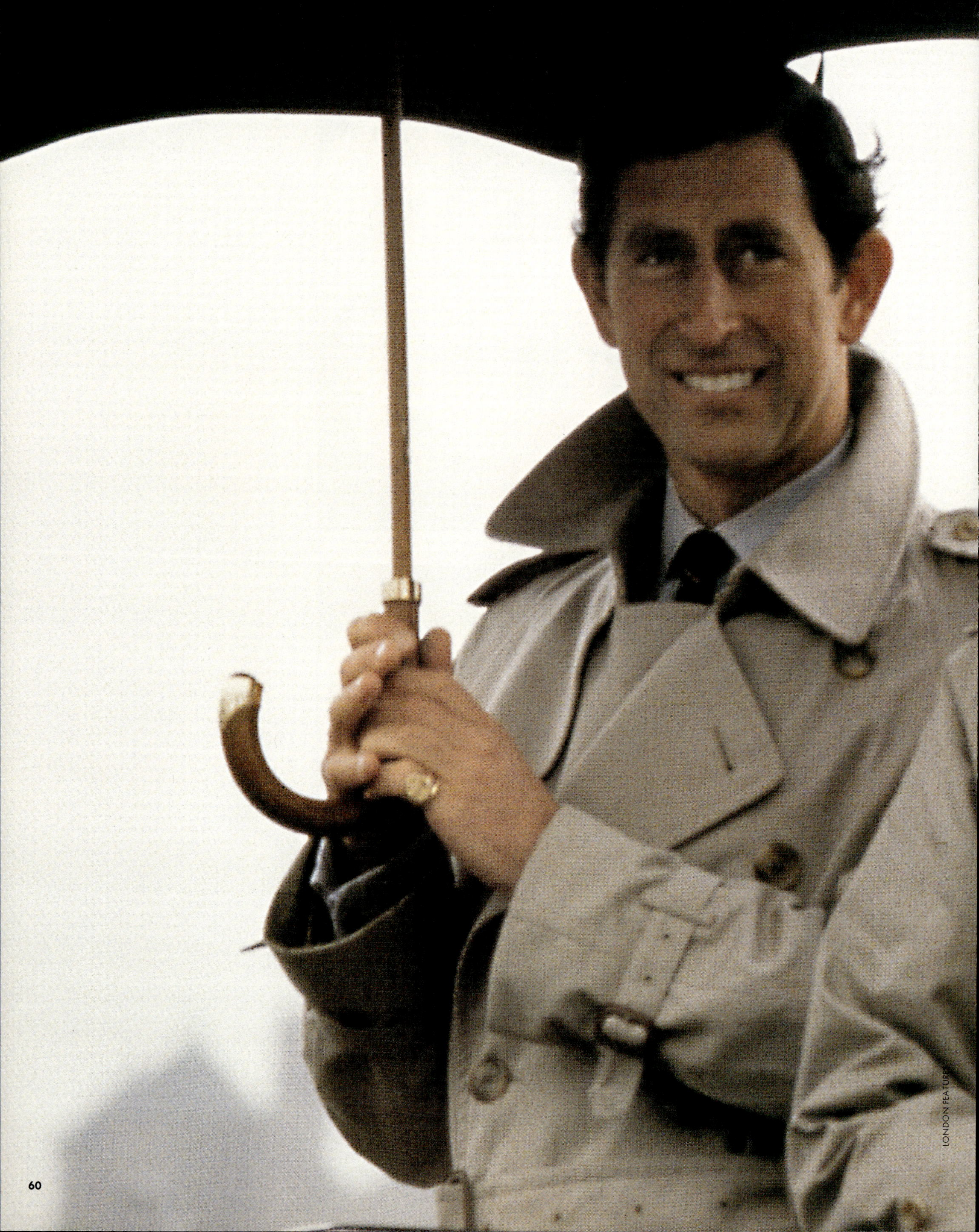

LONDON FEATURES

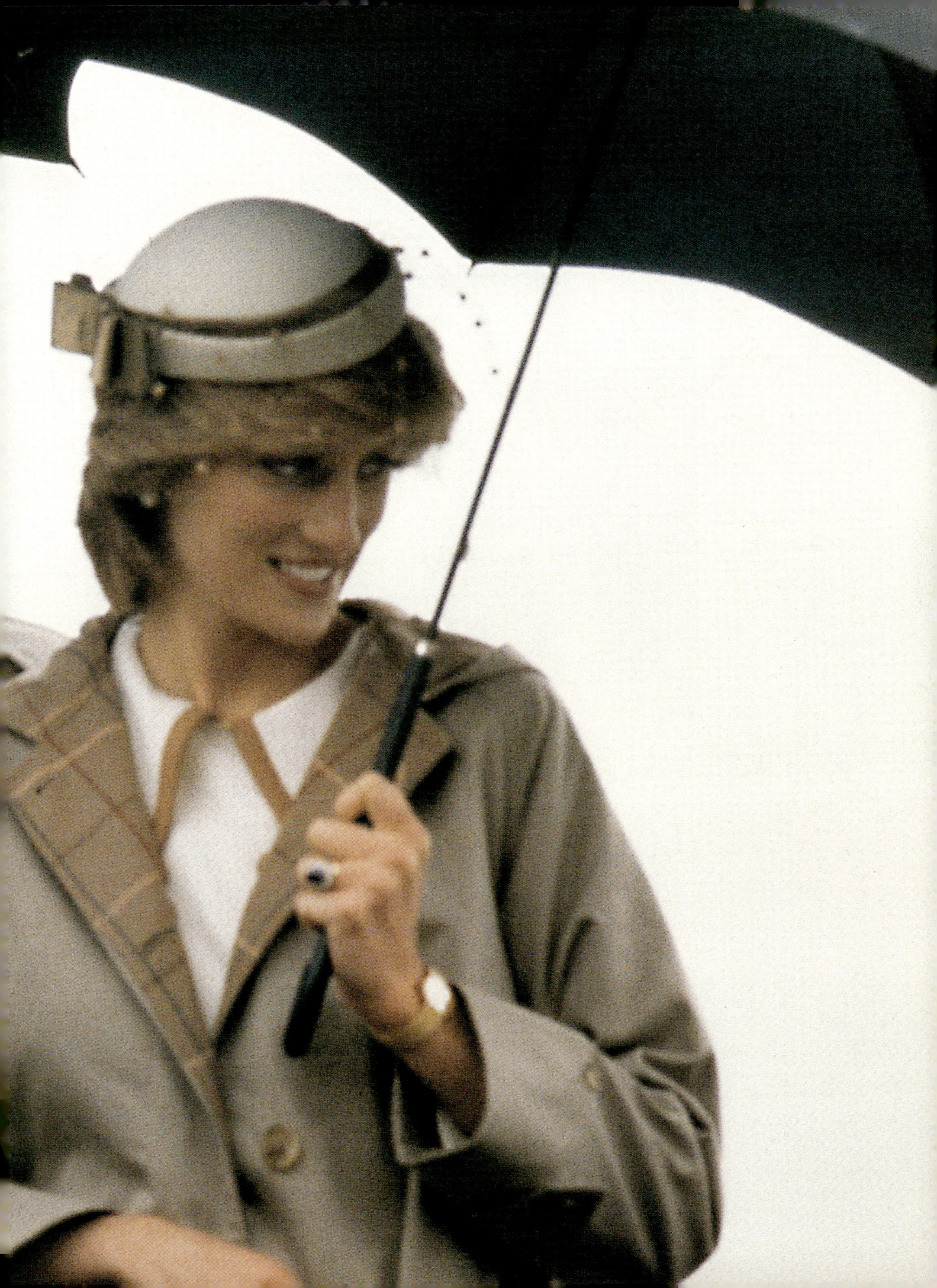

"We do this sort of thing rather well..."
—Prince Charles

FROM LEFT: TIM ANDERSON, ALPHA LONDON, BRENDAN BEIRNE REX USA, LTD.

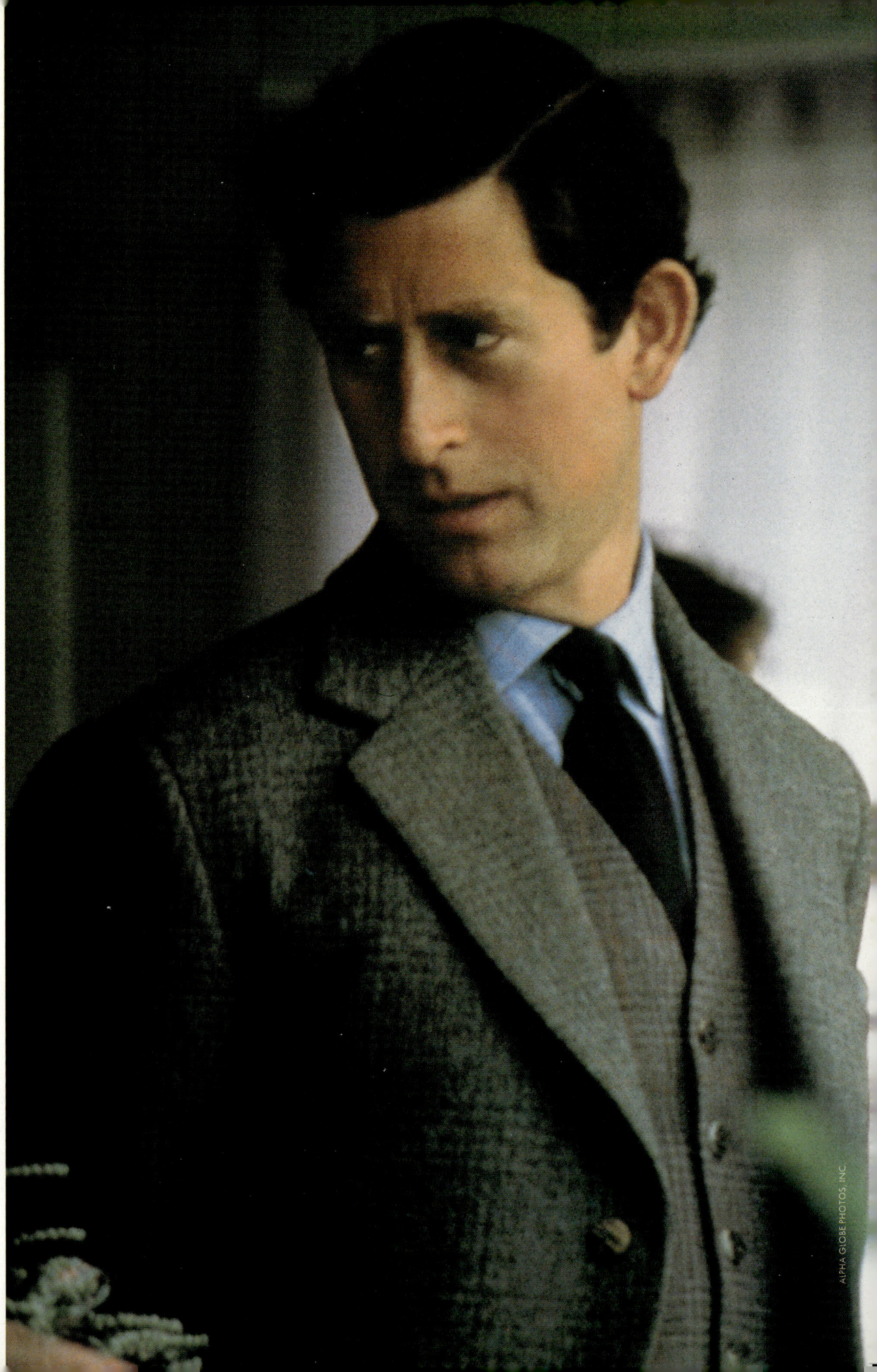
ALPHA GLOBE PHOTOS, INC.

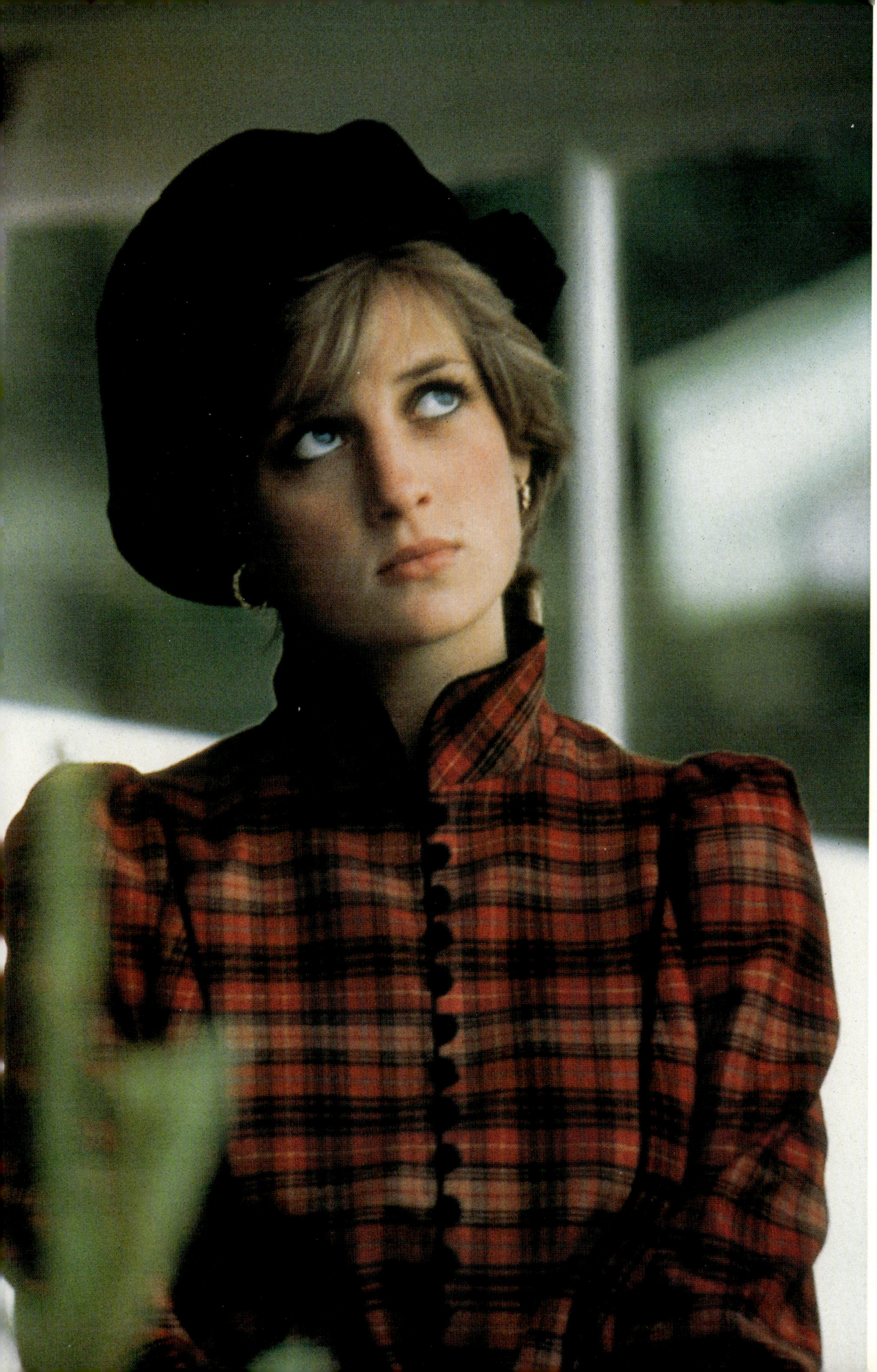

"We were a couple

which is very diffi

doing the same job,

cult for anyone...."

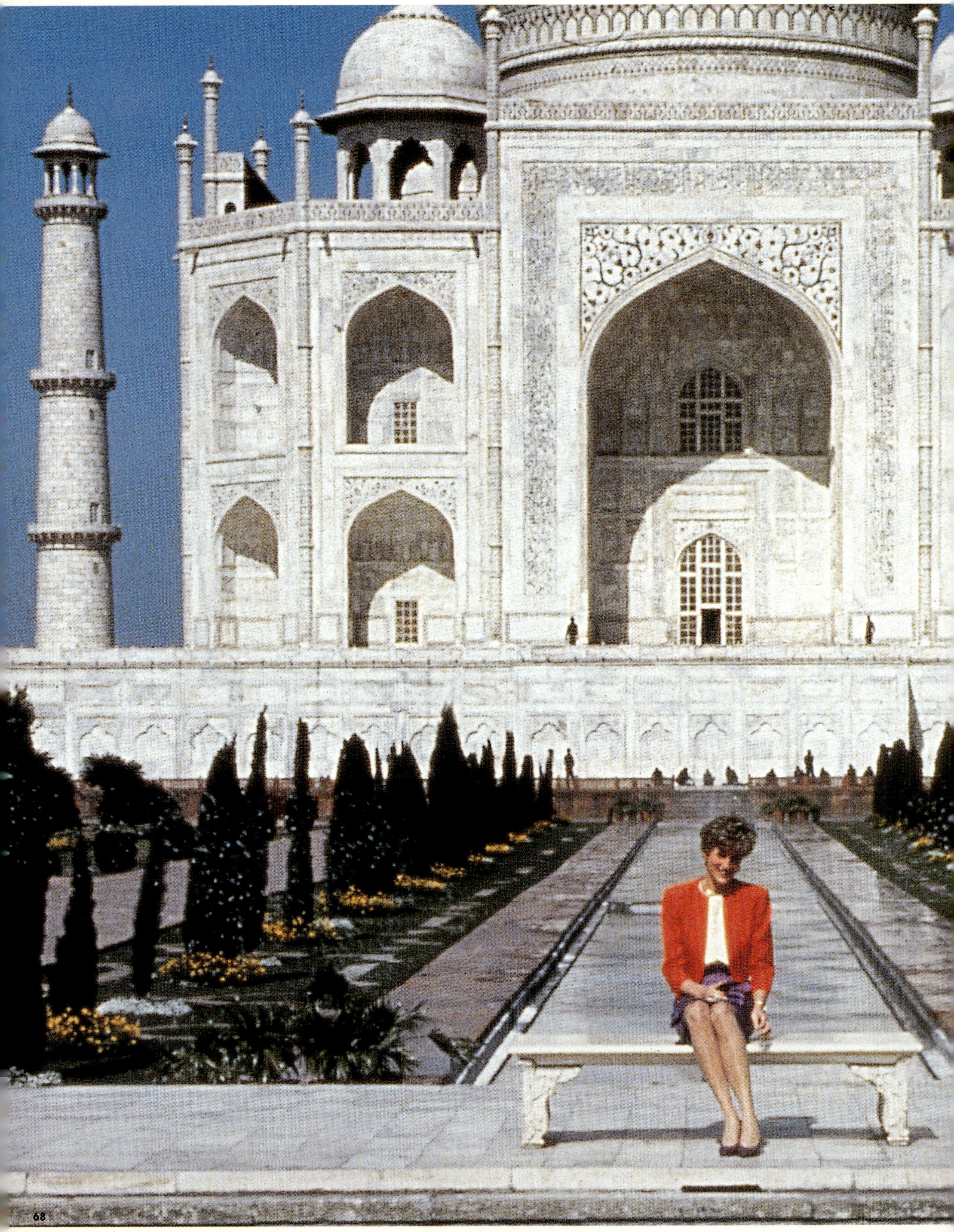

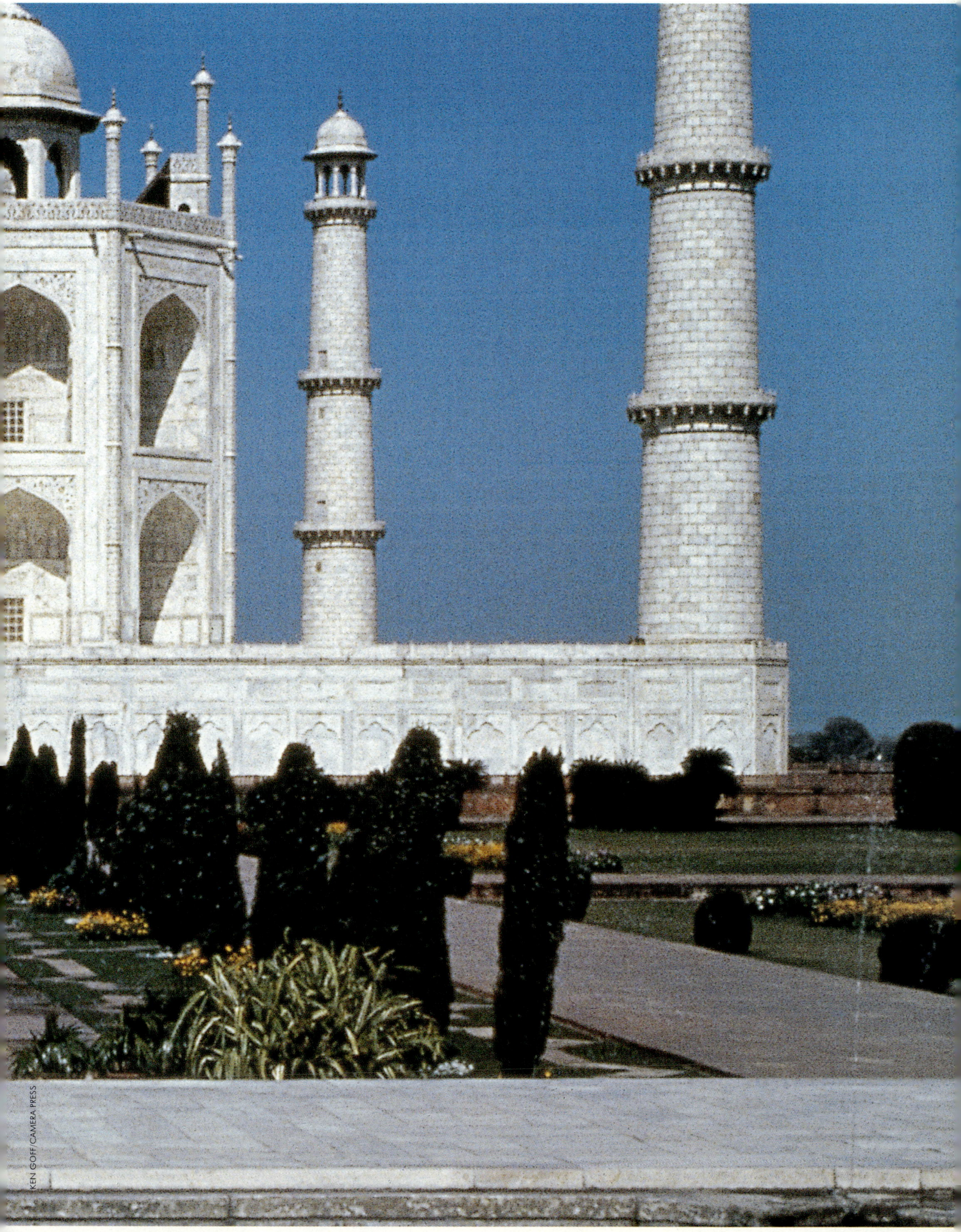

KEN GOFF/CAMERA PRESS

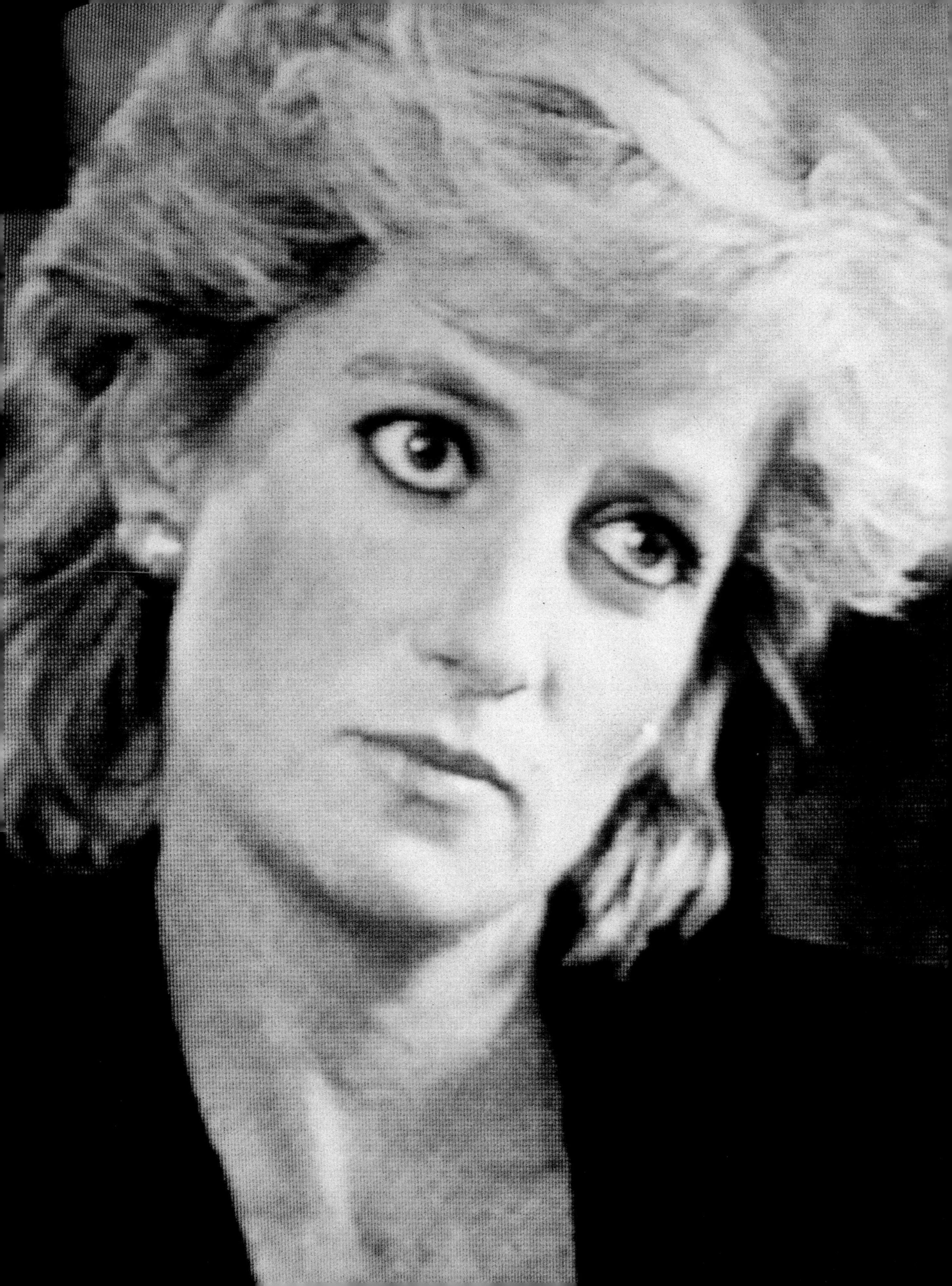

"I take some responsibility that our marriage went the way it did. I'll take half of it, but I won't take any more than that...."

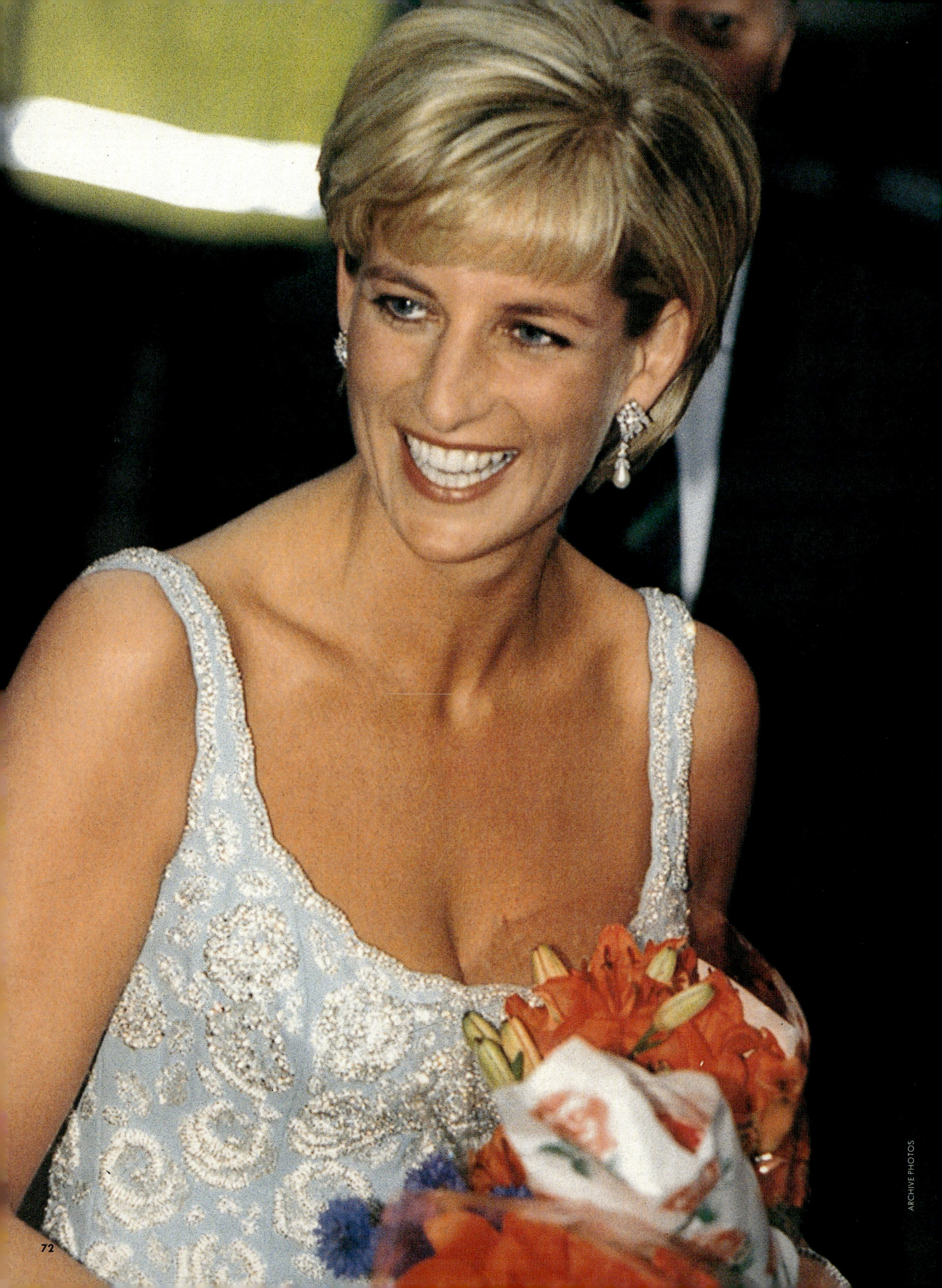

ARCHIVE PHOTOS

Queen of Hearts

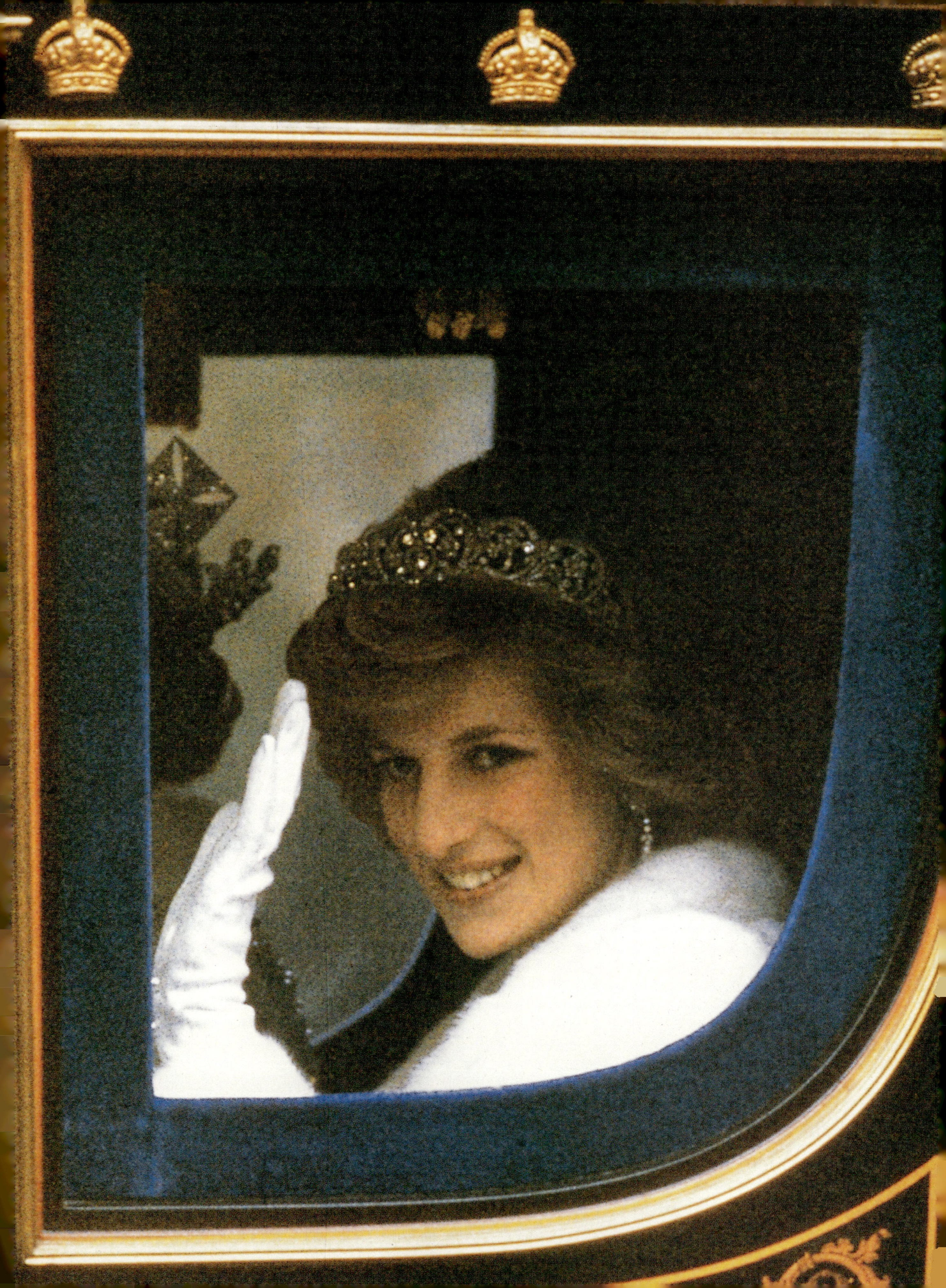

"I've always been the eighteen-year-old girl [Charles] got engaged to... my goodness, I've had to grow."

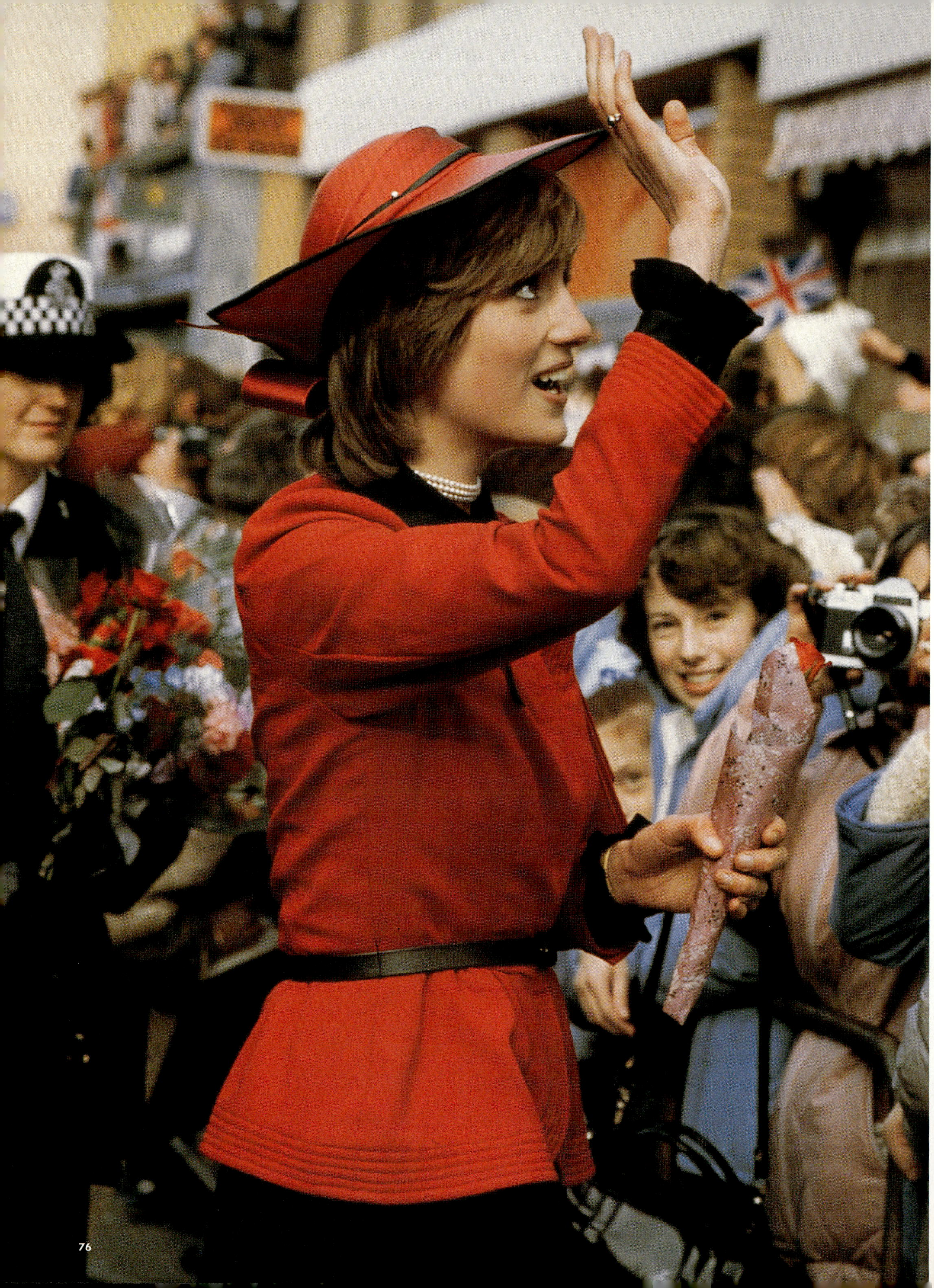

FROM LEFT: TIM GRAHAM/SYGMA, LONDON FEATURES INTERNATIONAL LTD

78

FROM LEFT: GAMMA LIAISON; DAVID HARTLEY/REX USA LTD.

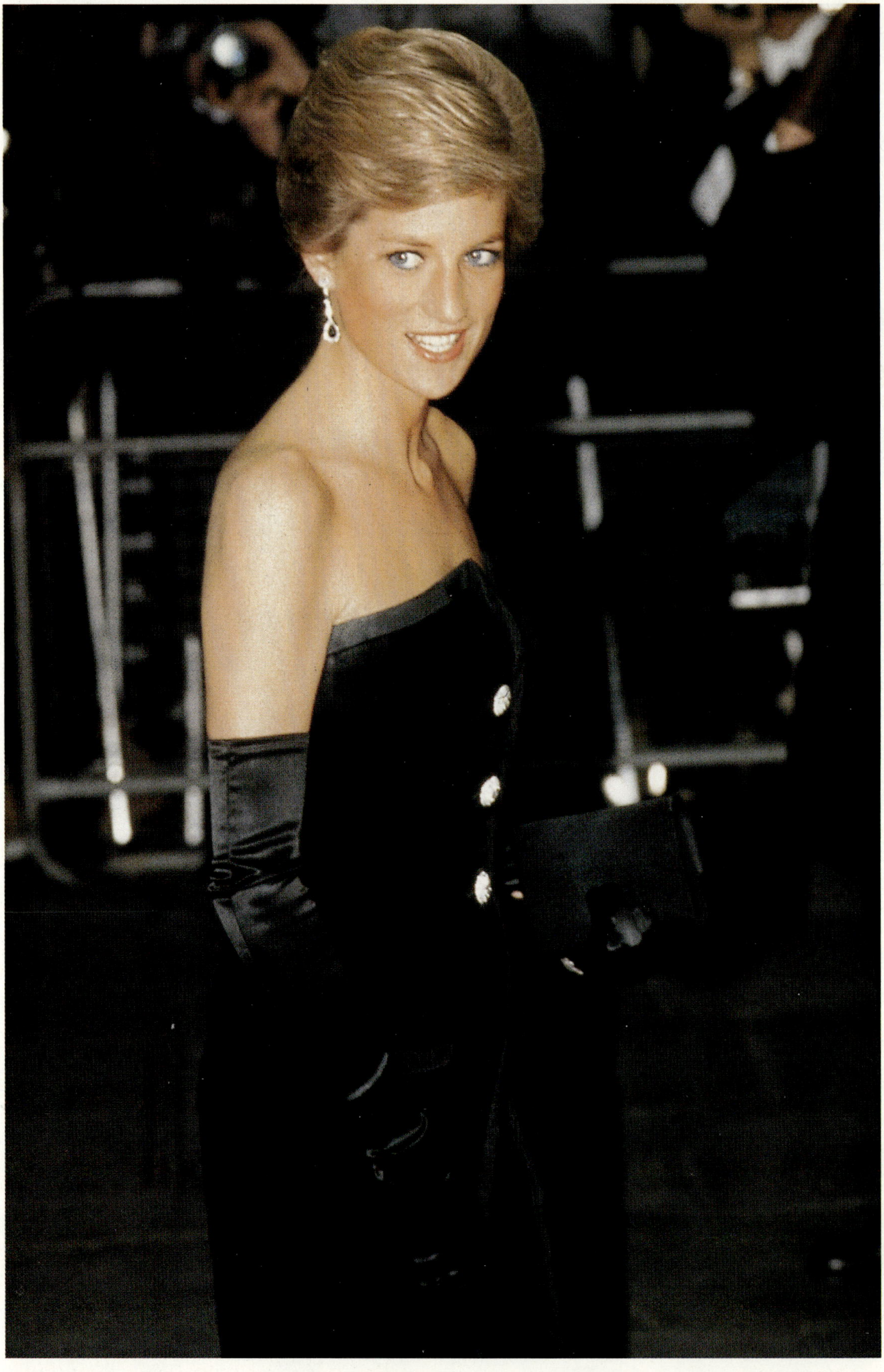

FROM LEFT: DAVID FISHER/LFI/LONDON FEATURES, PHIL LOFTUS/LONDON FEATURES.

82

KEN GOFF/GLOBE PHOTOS

"It was just the two of them dancing, and it was beautiful to behold. They were marvelous together."

—Nancy Reagan

FROM LEFT: CHERRUAULT/SIPA PRESS; ARCHIVE PHOTOS.

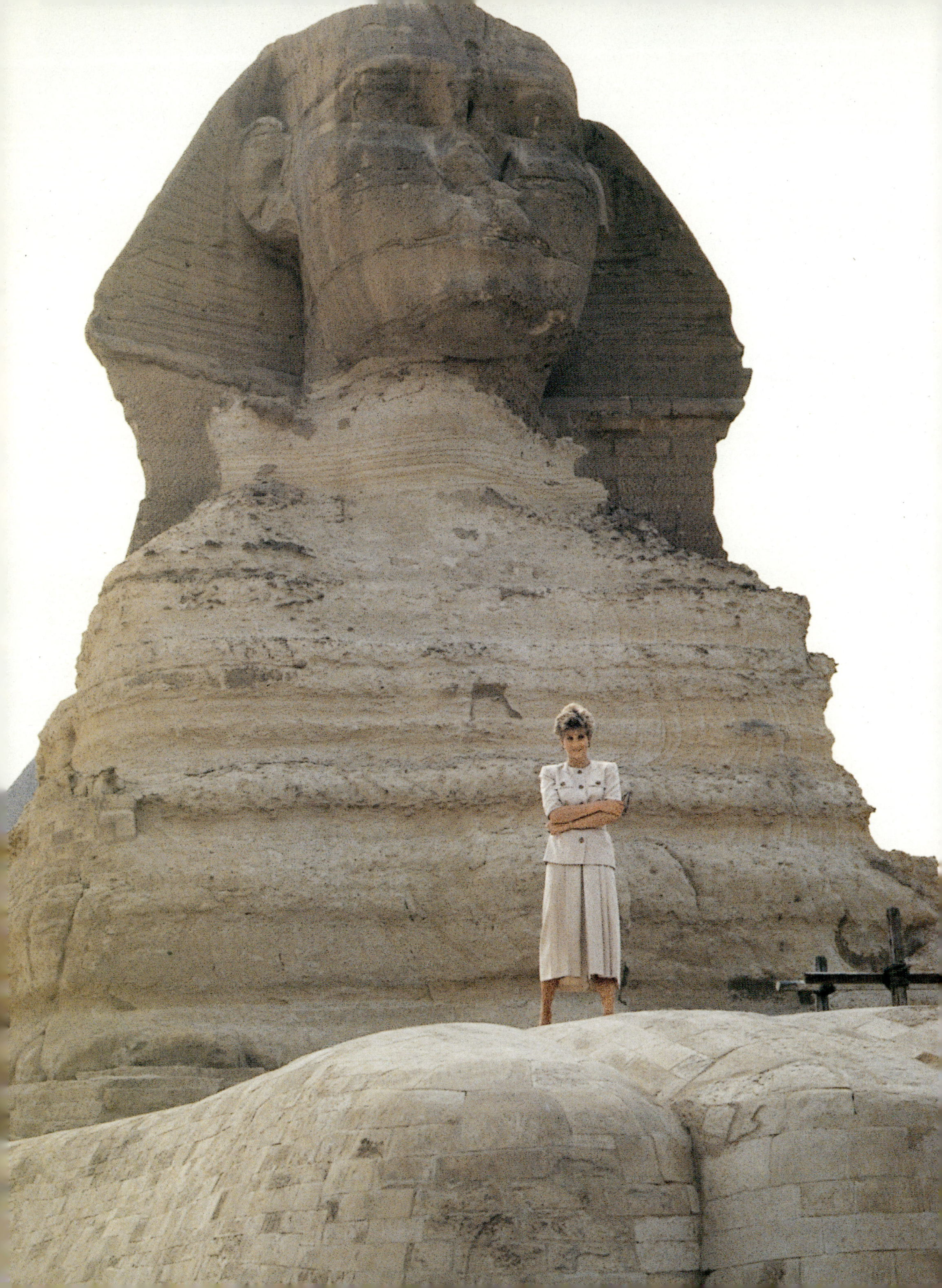

FROM LEFT: GLENN HARVEY/STILLS/RETNA LTD., CP/GLOBE PHOTOS INC./KEN GOFF.

87

"I haven't felt this free

since I was nineteen."

TOPHAM-PA/THE IMAGE WORKS

"*Your wonderfully mischievous sense of humor with the laugh that bent you double...*"

—*Earl Spencer, Diana's brother*

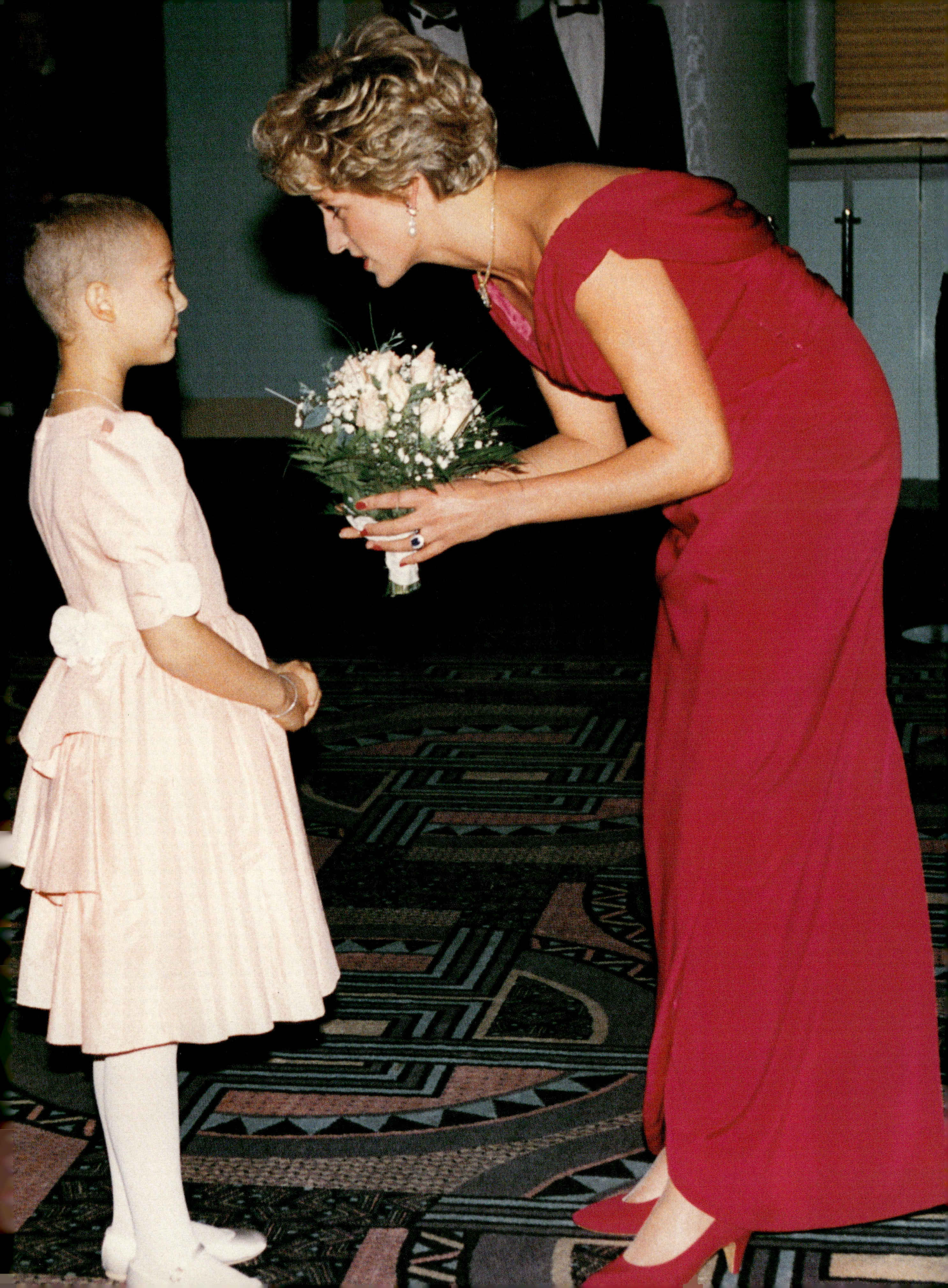

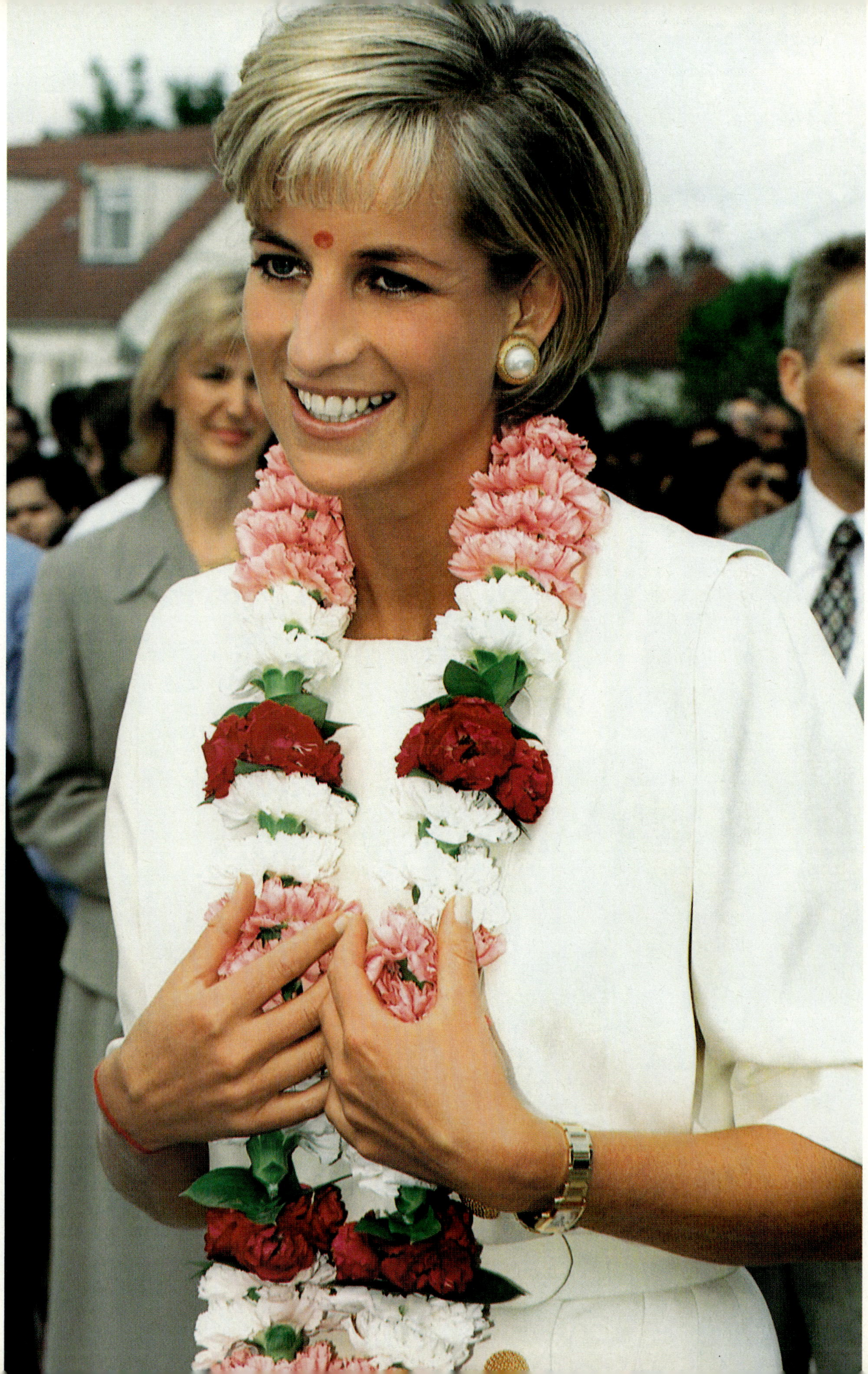

FROM LEFT: TOPHAM-PA/THE IMAGE WORKS, UPPA/IPOL, INC.

94

"Diana was the very essence of style…"

—*Earl Spencer, Diana's brother*

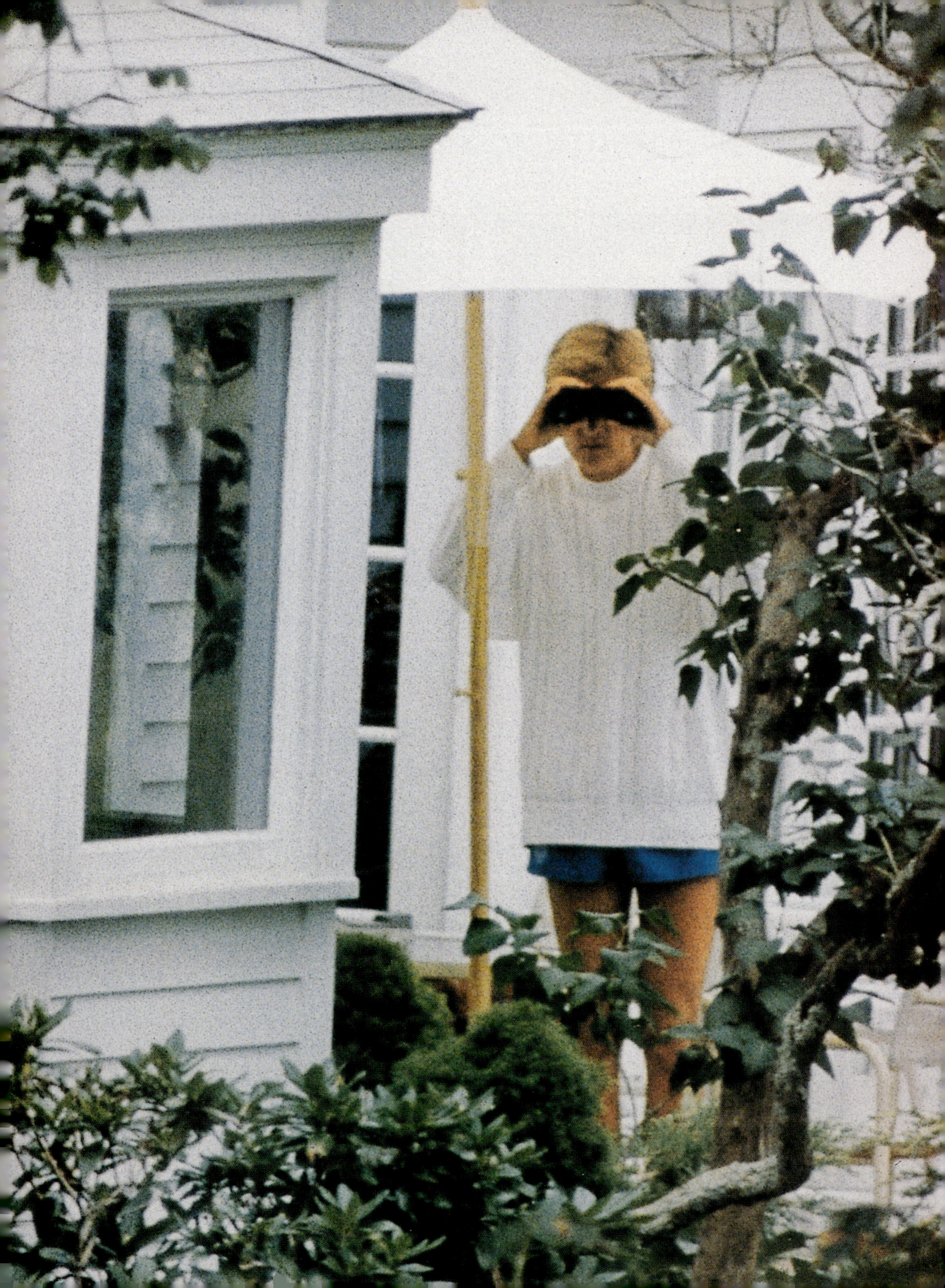

97

"How many times shall we remember her, in how many different ways—with the sick, the dying, with children, with the needy?"

—*Prime Minister Tony Blair*

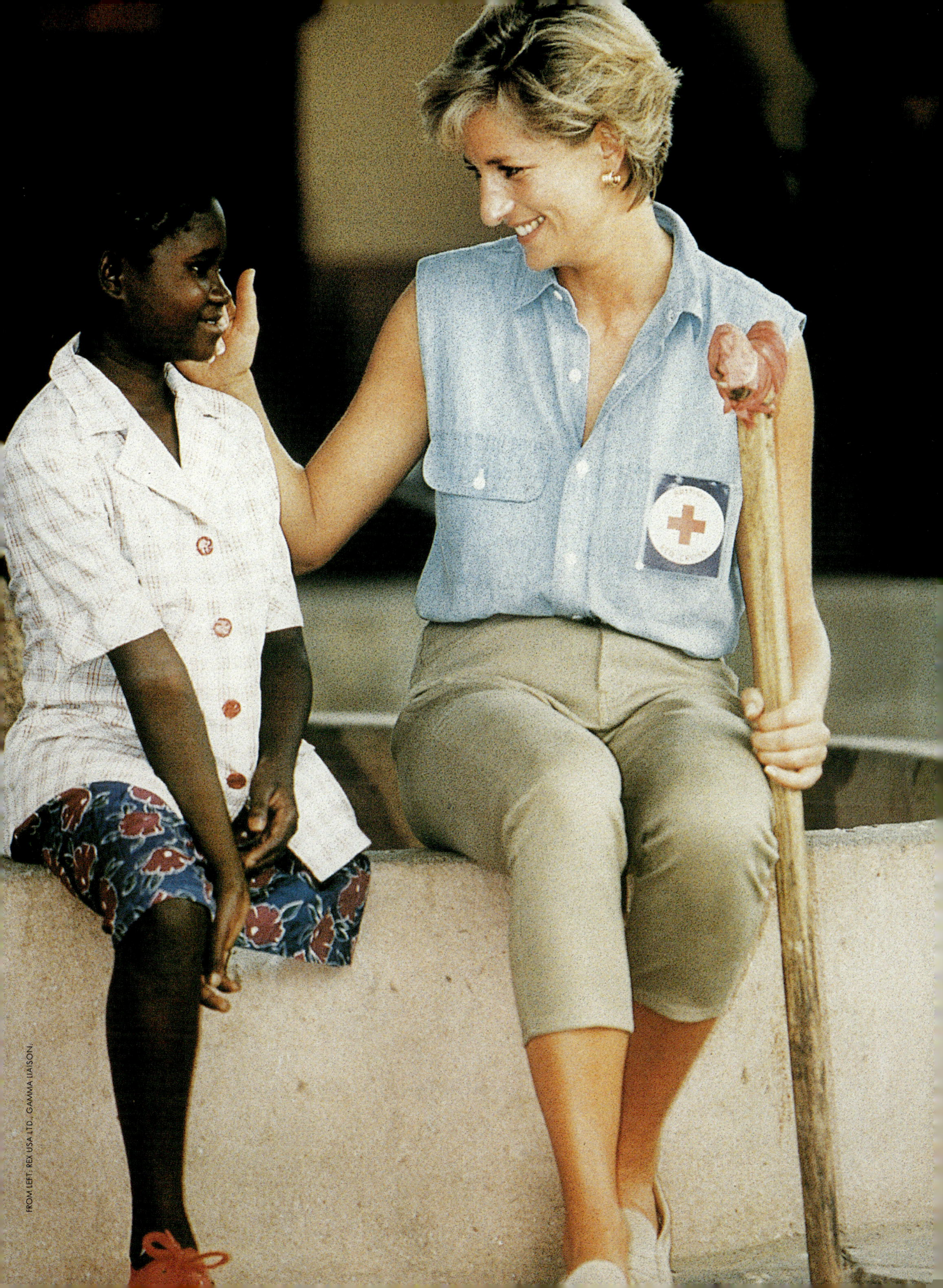

FROM LEFT: REX USA LTD.; GAMMA LIAISON.

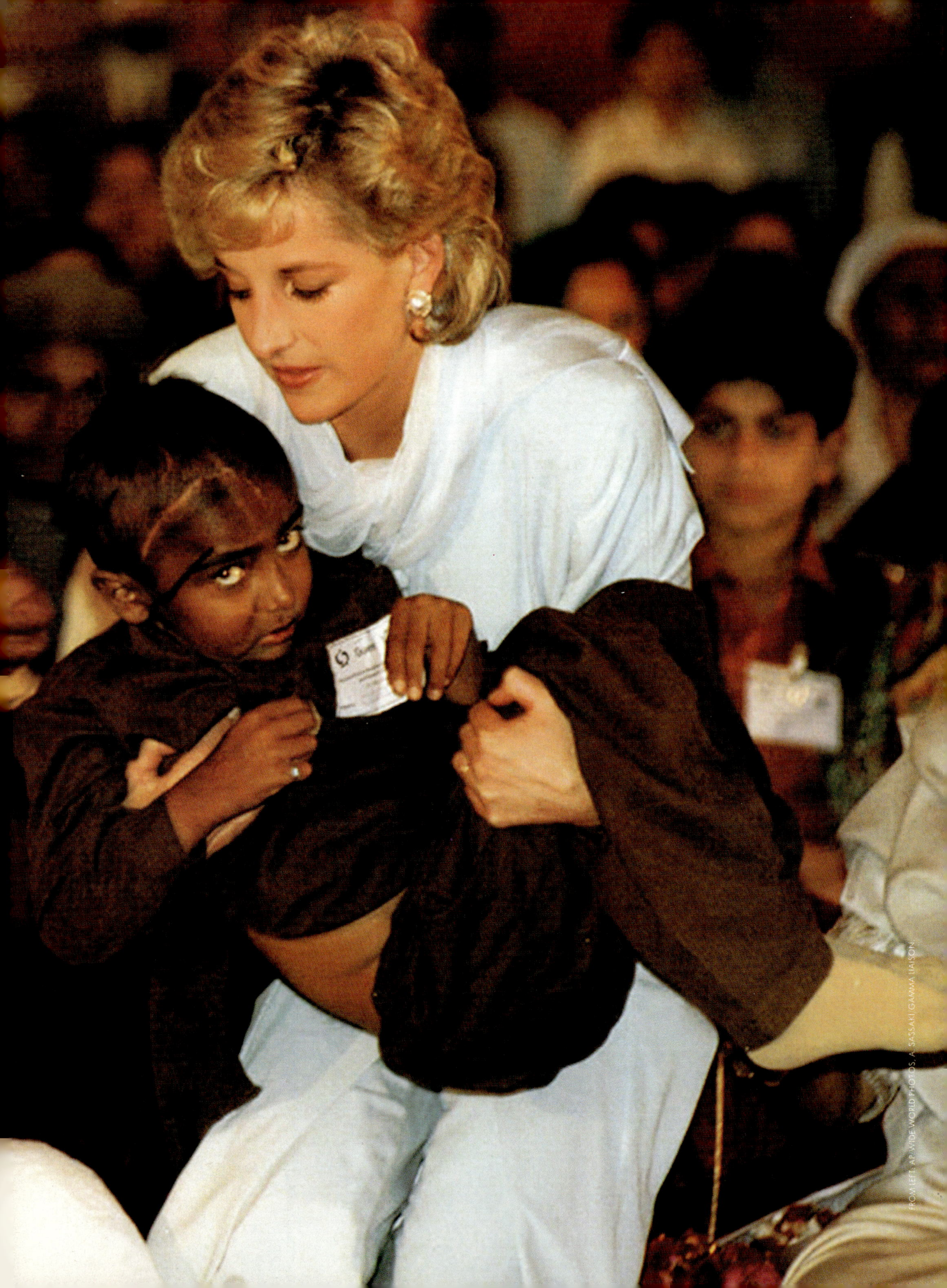

FROM LEFT: AP/WIDE WORLD PHOTOS; A. SASSAKI/GAMMA LIAISON.

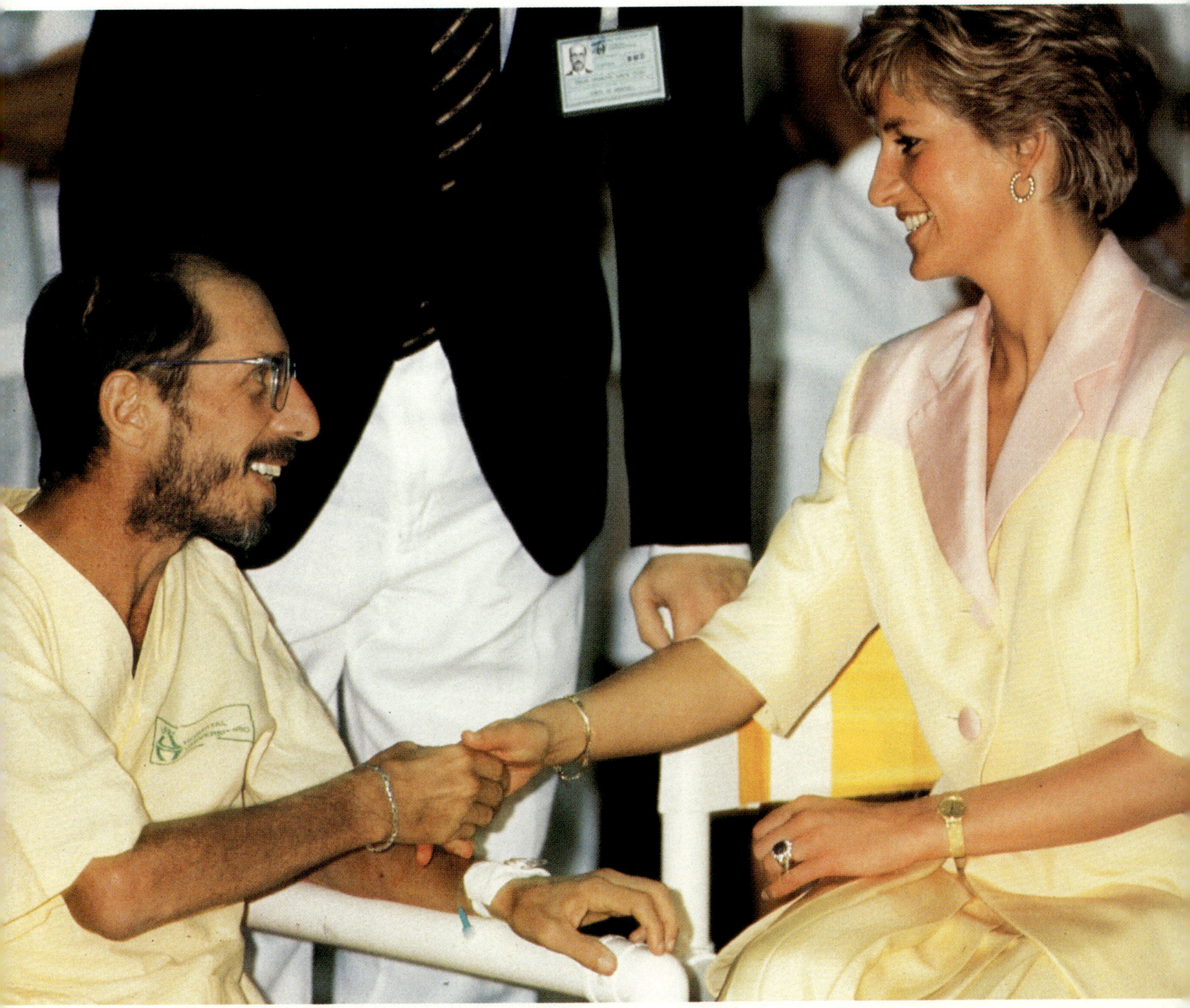

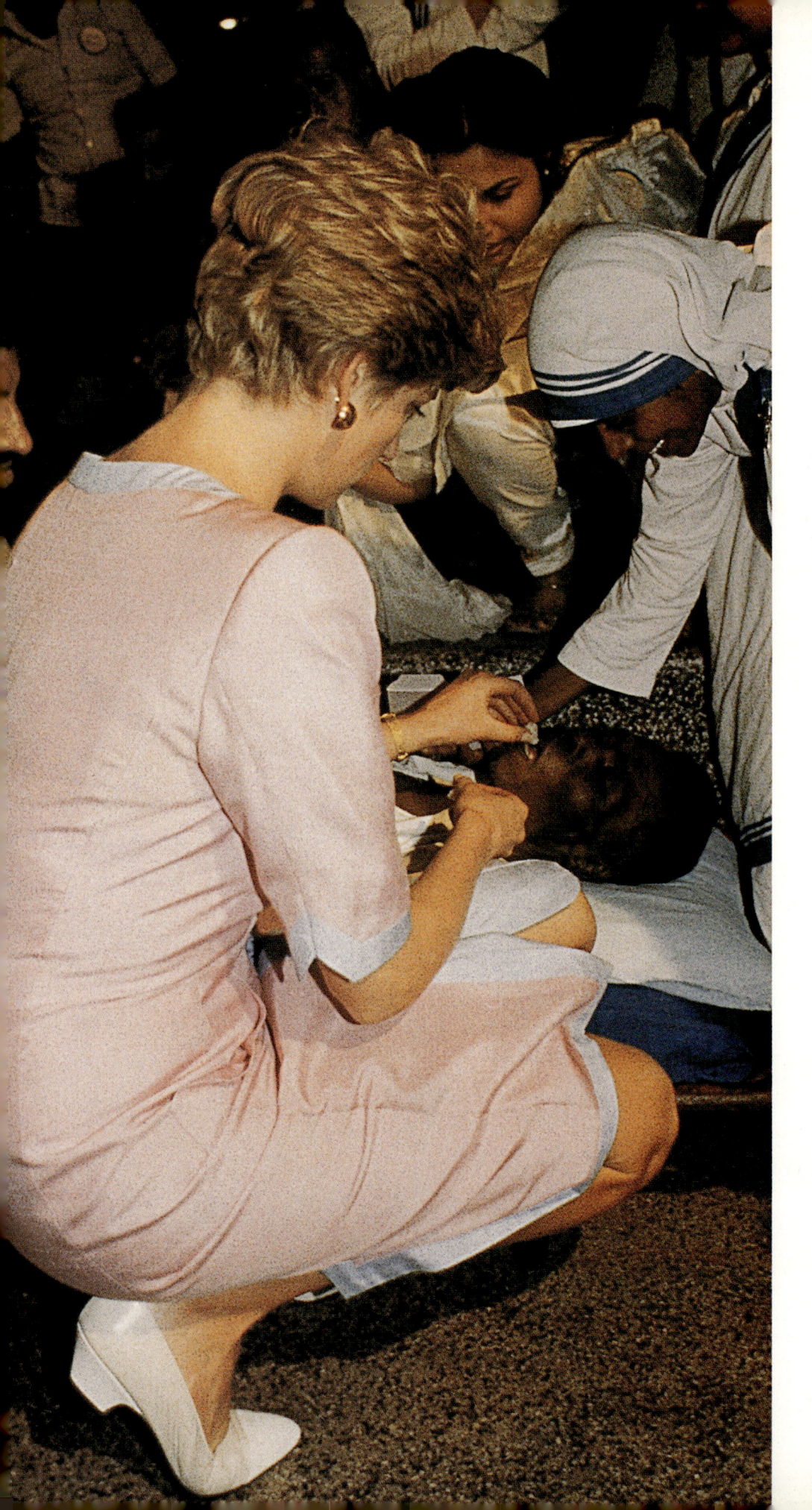

"She had a great love for the poor. She was very anxious to help me..."

—*Mother Teresa*

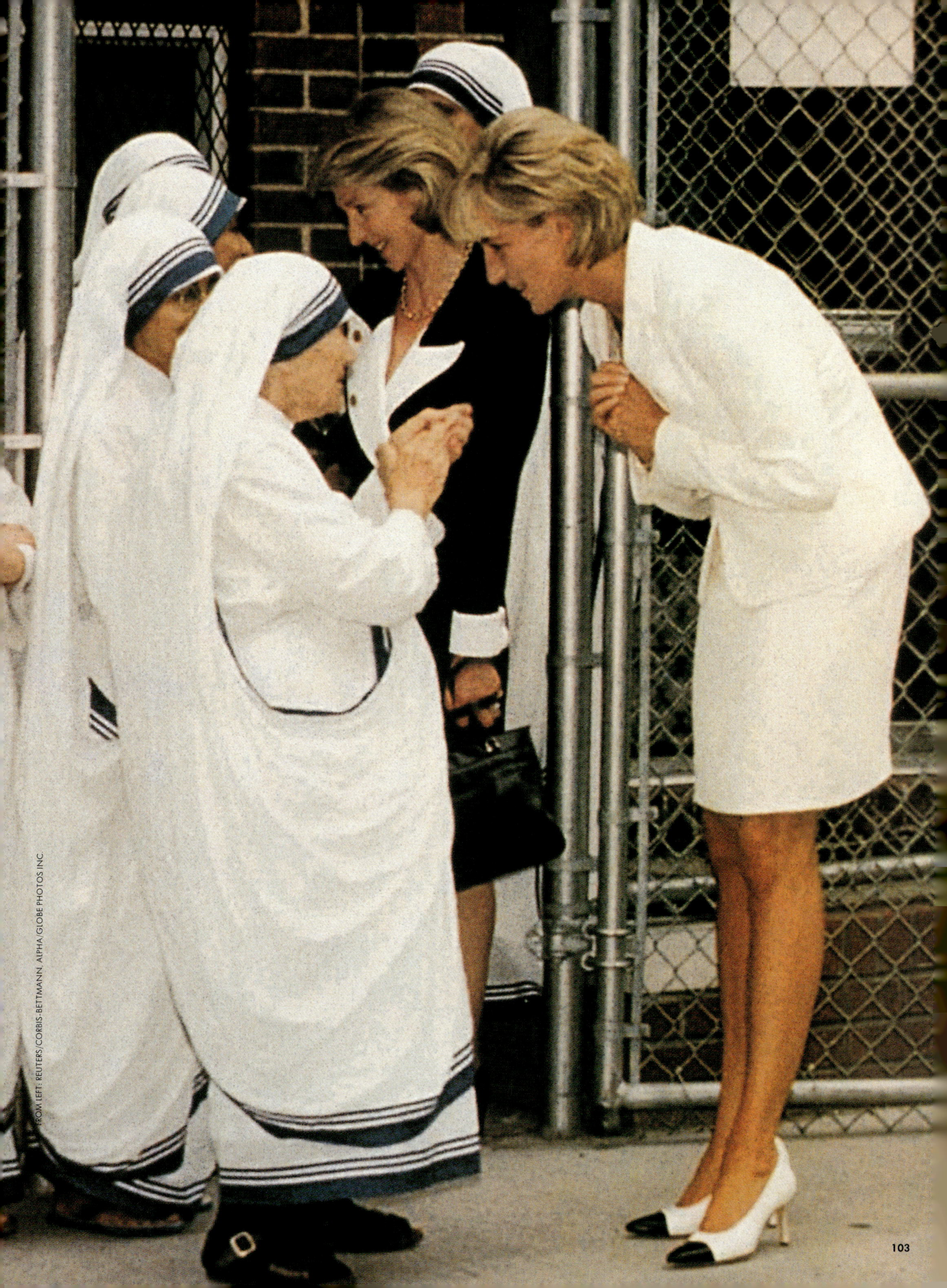

FROM LEFT: REUTERS/CORBIS-BETTMANN, ALPHA/GLOBE PHOTOS INC.

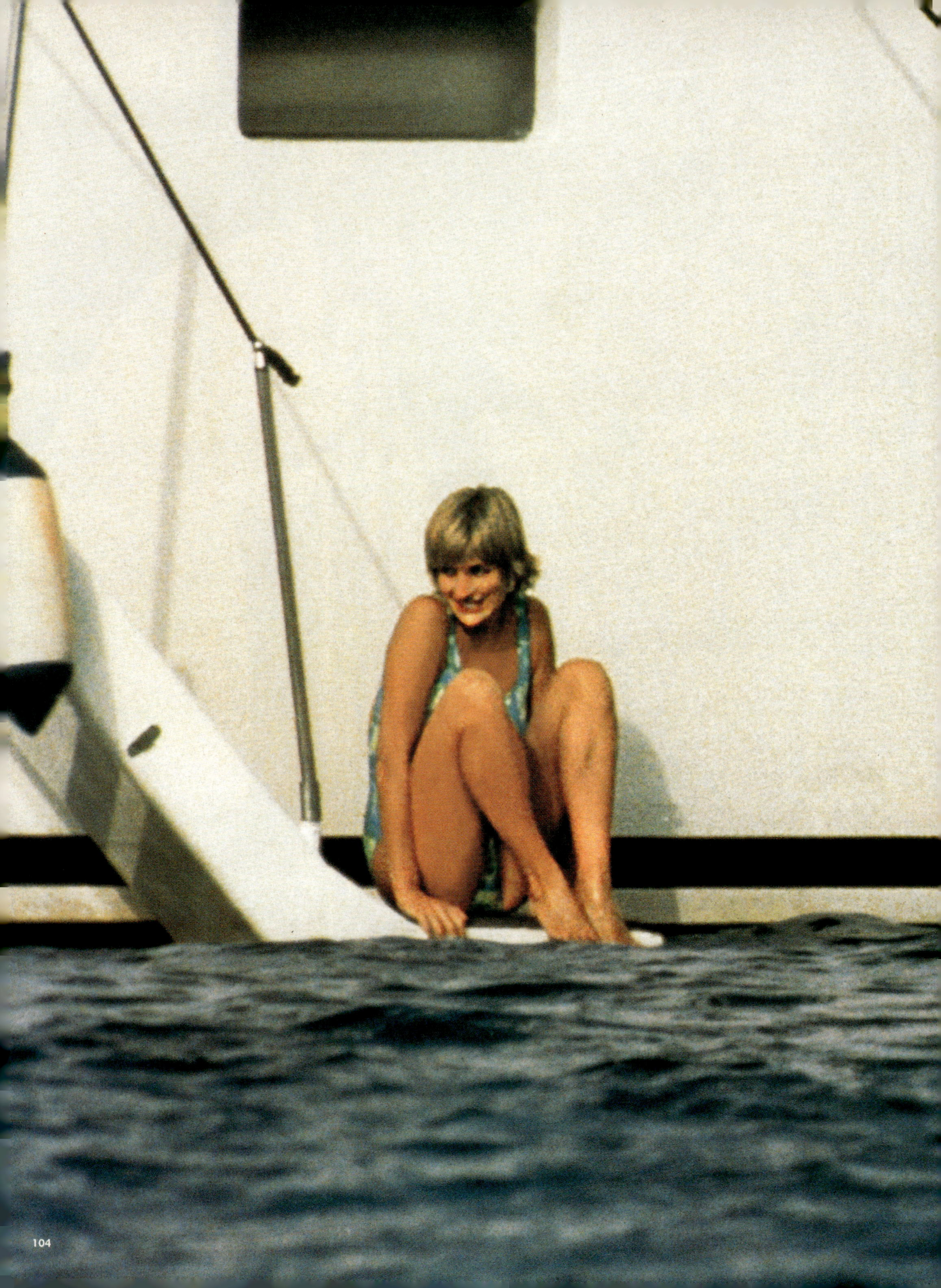

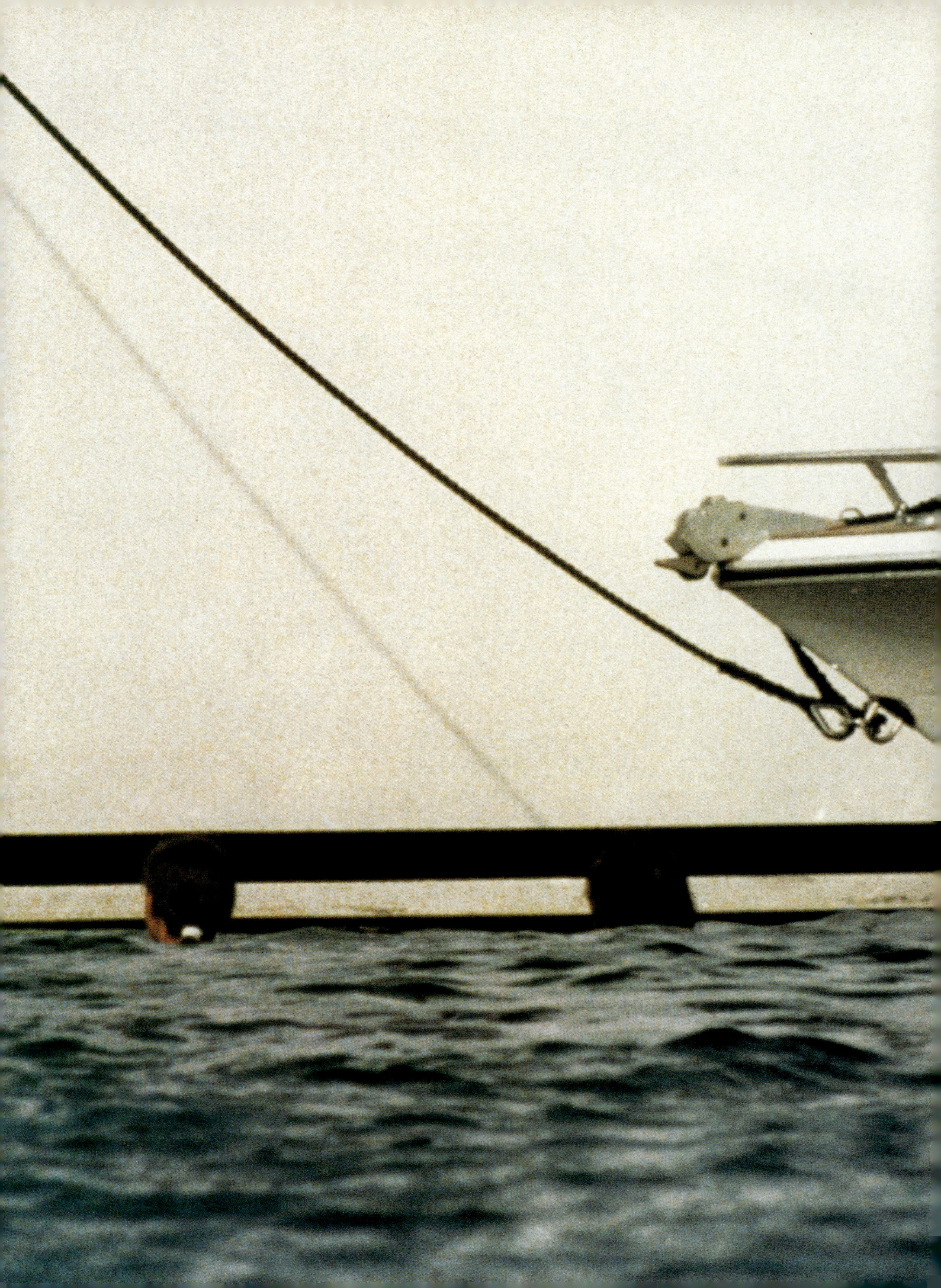

CLOCKWISE FROM LEFT: GIBOUX GAMMA LIAISON; KARIN COOPER GAMMA LIAISON; TIM GRAHAM SYGMA

"I've got my work that I choose to do, and I've got my boys…"

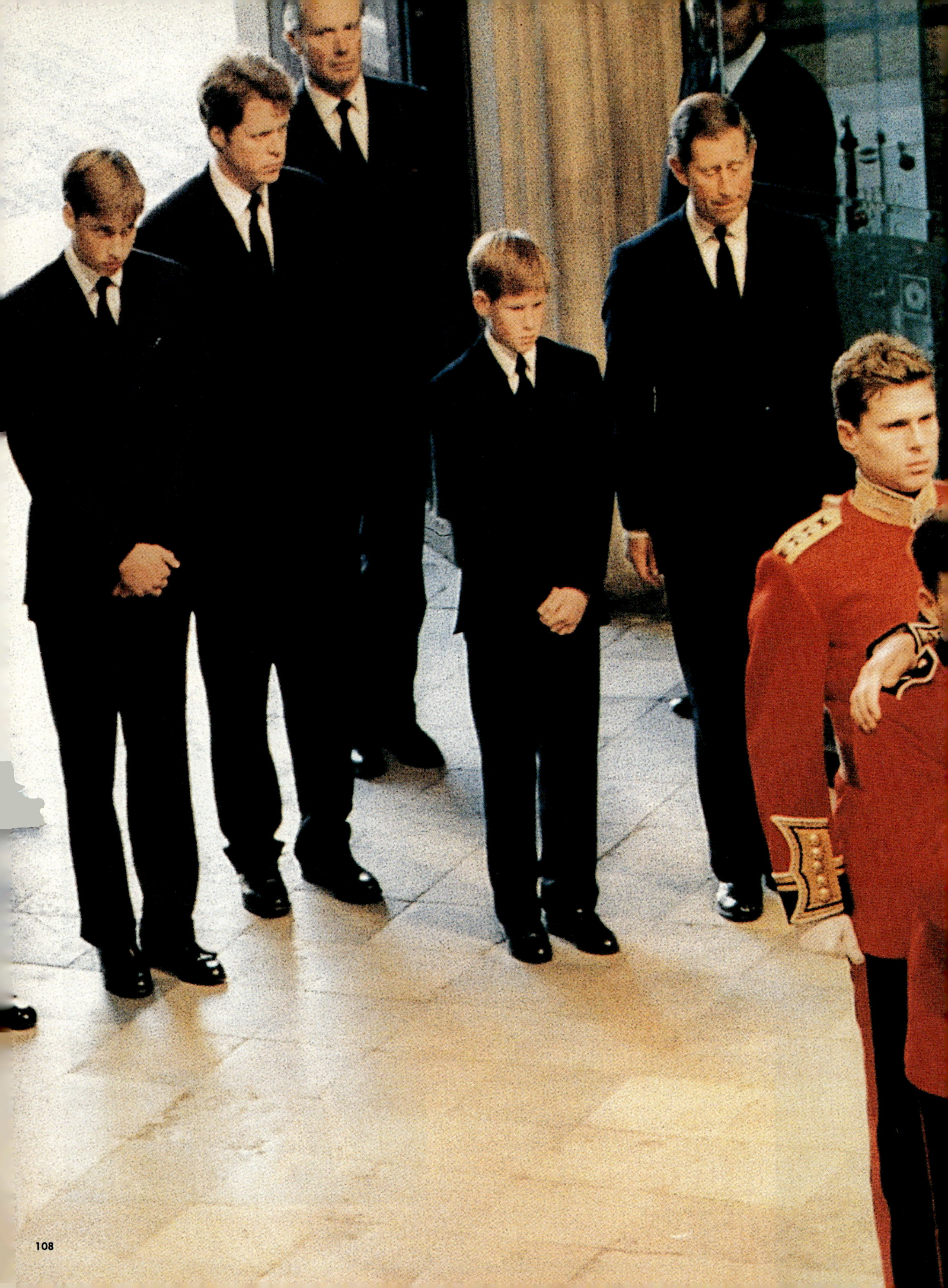

Time is too slow for those who wait, too swift for those who fear, too long for those who grieve, too short for those who rejoice, but for those who love, time is eternity.

—Anonymous, read at Diana's funeral service by Lady Jane Fellowes, her sister

"William knows how much Diana would want him to do the job he was born to do. He will be conscious of that, and, in her memory, do it even better." —*Lord Jeffrey Archer*

Myrna Blyth, Editor-in-Chief & Publishing Director
Carolyn Noyes, Managing Editor   Anna Demchick, Design Director   Chantal Belsheim, Photo Editor

Meredith CORPORATION

Chairman Jack D. Rehm
President & Chief Executive Officer William T. Kerr
President, Publishing Group Christopher M. Little

Chairman of the Executive Committee E.T. Meredith, III

© 1997 Meredith Corporation. All rights reserved. "Never Underestimate the Power of a Woman," "Can This Marriage Be Saved?" and "LHJ" are trademarks of Meredith Corporation, registered at U.S. Patent and Trademark Office. Title "Ladies' Home Journal" registered at U.S. Patent and Trademark Office and foreign countries. Printed in the U.S.A.